As one of the world's longest establi[shed]
and best-known travel bra[nds],
Thomas Cook are the experts in tr[avel].

For more than 135 years [our]
guidebooks have unlocked the se[crets]
of destinations around the w[orld]
sharing with travellers a wealth [of]
experience and a passion for travel.

**Rely on Thomas Cook as your
travelling companion on your next trip
and benefit from our unique heritage.**

Thomas Cook **traveller** guides

LAS VEGAS
Julie Mundy

Written by Julie Mundy, updated by Mike Gerrard and Donna Dailey
Original photography by Ethel Davies

Published by Thomas Cook Publishing
A division of Thomas Cook Tour Operations Limited.
Company registration no. 3772199 England
The Thomas Cook Business Park, Unit 9, Coningsby Road,
Peterborough PE3 8SB, United Kingdom
Email: books@thomascook.com, Tel: + 44 (0) 1733 416477
www.thomascookpublishing.com

Produced by Cambridge Publishing Management Limited
Burr Elm Court, Main Street, Caldecote CB23 7NU
www.cambridgepm.co.uk

ISBN: 978-1-84848-322-4

© 2004, 2006, 2008 Thomas Cook Publishing
This fourth edition © 2010
Text © Thomas Cook Publishing
Maps © Thomas Cook Publishing

Series Editor: Karen Beaulah
Production/DTP: Steven Collins

Printed and bound in Spain by GraphyCems

Cover photography: © GlowCam/SIME

Contents

Introduction

Las Vegas is the ultimate city of excess – a 21st-century city where you can take a global journey through time and space just by walking a few short kilometres of the Las Vegas Strip. No other city can offer you ancient Rome, Paris, Venice, medieval England, Hollywood or the Far East, all captured within the largest and most luxurious hotels in the world.

When people think of Las Vegas, many envision European-style resorts with glamorous titles such as Bellagio, The Venetian or the Monte Carlo, while others just see glittering façades over a disorderly gambling town. Gaudy or refined, fairy tale or fake, Las Vegas is recognised the world over for its imposing neon architecture, ostentatious showmen and no-limits gambling, and has been described by the *Los Angeles Times* as 'the last great mythic city that western civilisation will ever create'.

The city's attraction is evident in its visitor statistics. With over 150,000 hotel rooms (and rising, even in the recession), and almost 20,000 conventions held there every year, Las Vegas is a leading tourist attraction in the United States, with a county gaming industry worth almost $9 billion a year.

With more hotel rooms than Orlando or Los Angeles, more than 36 million visitors are seduced by Las Vegas each year. Contrary to popular belief, the city has a greater attraction for tourism than for gamblers. The economic impact of all these wide-eyed visitors generates $30 billion in southern Nevada, with the city-wide attractions now overtaking the gaming tables for tourist appeal. Compare Las Vegas with Atlantic City: the east-coast city may achieve similar annual gaming revenues, but it only holds on to its average visitor for eight hours, while Las Vegas can attract you for days on end.

Its luminous enticement also ensures that over 80 per cent of those who visit Las Vegas will return. Devotees have come back year after year to see the city evolve: from a scattering of gambling rooms and dude ranches in the 1930s, to the growth of the Las Vegas Strip in the '40s, the glamour of the city in the atomic era of the '50s, through to the swinging '60s and beyond.

In the 1990s the Strip underwent a new construction boom, with the creation of themed hotels such as

Treasure Island, with its own pirate-ship battle, and the tropical paradise of Mandalay Bay, followed by the glorious cityscapes of New York, Paris and Venice. The new millennium ushered in the era of the mega resort with the opening of the theatrical Bellagio with its operatic fountains, and the sleek Wynn with its 'Lake of Dreams', not to mention its own luxury car dealership. Vegas continues to raise the stakes for unbridled extravagance and scale with MGM's $9.2 billion CityCenter, opening in 2009, a 27-hectare (67-acre) resort that includes its own power plant and fire station.

From a small oasis within the desert mountains, Las Vegas has grown into the largest US city born after 1900. In 2008 the population exceeded two million and residents are committed to transforming the city from a circus act into a dynamic lifestyle city. As for its visitors, seduced by A-list headliners, Hollywood celebrities, fine dining and entertainment, it is no wonder that millions of people return to Las Vegas every year.

Introduction

The southern end of the Las Vegas Strip

The city

This city is far more than the Las Vegas Strip. Many package holidays transport you directly from the airport to the Strip, and it is also the first area you will encounter on the long desert drive from Los Angeles; but if this is all you experience, then you really have missed Las Vegas.

Downtown Las Vegas, the Hoover Dam and the Grand Canyon – the creations of man and nature – can often remain unseen. With the Strip being so enticing, it is hard to imagine there is more beyond the neon.

The Las Vegas Strip

The area of Las Vegas Boulevard running from Mandalay Bay to Charleston Boulevard (just beyond the Stratosphere Tower) is known as the Strip. Over the years this road had several names, from the Arrowhead Highway to the Salt Lake or Los Angeles Highway, before it was christened Las Vegas Boulevard South. It was nicknamed 'the Strip' by Police Captain Guy McAfee, who owned the Pair-O-Dice club on this highway before it was populated by casinos.

Downtown

North of Charleston Boulevard is Downtown Las Vegas. This is the original casino centre, where Las Vegas first developed. It is now a pedestrianised area, and home to the spectacular Fremont Street Experience.

How to see Las Vegas

The Strip is easy to walk around, although during the summer your main obstacle may be the heat. The Strip has six lanes of busy traffic, but offers wide pavements and several crossing points and bridges for pedestrians, while downtown Fremont Street is completely free of traffic.

Some hotels also have moving walkways into their entrances, and there are lifts and escalators servicing the bridges over the Strip, which even the keenest of walkers will find themselves using after a couple of days on their feet.

Buses operate from the Downtown Transportation Center on Stewart Avenue, running down the Strip to cover most of the hotels every ten minutes, stopping at the CAT (Citizens Area Transit) bus stops, while off-Strip

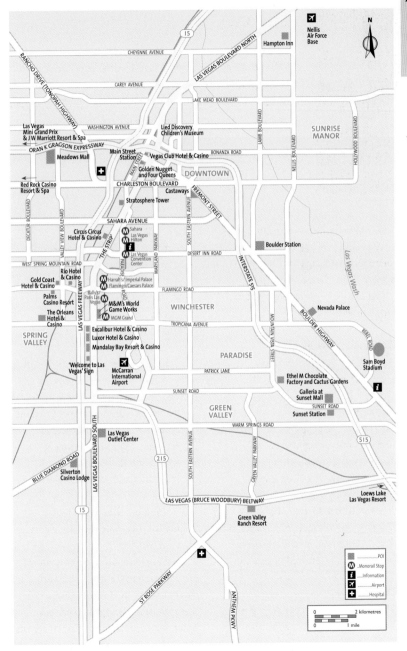

Nellis
Air Force
Base

Hampton Inn

N

CHEYENNE AVENUE

RANCHO DRIVE (TONOPAH HIGHWAY)

CAREY AVENUE

LAKE MEAD BOULEVARD

LAS VEGAS BOULEVARD NORTH

LAMB BOULEVARD

NELLIS BOULEVARD

HOLLYWOOD BOULEVARD

SUNRISE
MANOR

Las Vegas
Mini Grand Prix
& J W Marriott Resort & Spa

WASHINGTON AVENUE

Lied Discovery
Children's Museum

ORAN K GRAGSON EXPRESSWAY

Meadows Mall

Main Street
Station

MAIN STREET

Vegas Club Hotel & Casino

BONANZA ROAD

Golden Nugget
and Four Queens

DOWNTOWN

Red Rock Casino
Resort & Spa

CHARLESTON BOULEVARD

Castaways

FREMONT STREET

DECATUR BOULEVARD

VALLEY VIEW BOULEVARD

Stratosphere Tower

SOUTH EASTERN AVENUE

SAHARA AVENUE

Circus Circus
Hotel & Casino

THE STRIP

M Sahara
M Las Vegas
Hilton
i
M Las Vegas
Convention
Center

DESERT INN ROAD

INTERSTATE 515

Boulder Station

Las Vegas Wash

WEST SPRING MOUNTAIN ROAD

Rio Hotel
& Casino

Gold Coast
Hotel & Casino

M Harrah's/Imperial Palace
M Flamingo/Caesars Palace

FLAMINGO ROAD

Palms
Casino Resort

LAS VEGAS FREEWAY

Bally's/
Paris Las
Vegas

M M&M's World
Game Works
M MGM Grand

WINCHESTER

MOUNTAIN VISTA STREET

BOULDER HIGHWAY

Nevada Palace

REBEL ROAD

The Orleans
Hotel &
Casino

TROPICANA AVENUE

SPRING
VALLEY

Excalibur Hotel & Casino
Luxor Hotel & Casino
Mandalay Bay Resort & Casino

PARADISE

Sam Boyd
Stadium

i

'Welcome to Las
Vegas' Sign

McCarran
International
Airport

PATRICK LANE

Ethel M Chocolate
Factory and Cactus Gardens

SUNSET ROAD

Galleria at
Sunset Mall

GREEN
VALLEY

SUNSET ROAD

Sunset Station

WARM SPRINGS ROAD

LAS VEGAS BOULEVARD SOUTH

Las Vegas
Outlet Center

SOUTH EASTERN AVENUE

215

GREEN VALLEY PARKWAY

515

BLUE DIAMOND ROAD

Silverton
Casino Lodge

LAS VEGAS (BRUCE WOODBURY) BELTWAY

Loews Lake
Las Vegas Resort

15

Green Valley
Ranch Resort

ST ROSE PARKWAY

ANTHEM PKWY

POI
M Monorail Stop
i Information
Airport
Hospital

0   2 kilometres

0   1 mile

transfers are also available. The main route for visitors is the Deuce service, which runs from the South Strip transfer terminal, along the full length of the Strip to Downtown Las Vegas stopping at every hotel on the Strip. These striking silver double-decker buses hold 97 passengers and run 24 hours a day every 7–8 minutes during peak hours (10am–1am) and every 10–17 minutes at off-peak times (1am–10am).

The Las Vegas Strip trolley runs every 15 minutes from 8.30am until

Downtown Fremont Street, the original casino centre

midnight, stopping at the major hotels from the Stratosphere to Mandalay Bay, but, to avoid the traffic, the Strip also boasts four monorail services. The Las Vegas monorail runs from 7am until 2am Mon–Thur and until 3am Fri–Sun along the whole length of the Strip, from the MGM Grand to the Sahara. While you can buy single tickets for this service, it's far more economical to buy six rides at a time, or unlimited one- or three-day passes. Other monorails operate between Mirage and TI (from 9am until midnight), from Bellagio to Monte Carlo (24 hours), and from Mandalay Bay through Luxor to the Excalibur (24 hours).

Las Vegas also has an abundance of taxicabs. They can be found queuing outside the main entrance of most hotels, but the valet must call them over for you. Most taxis will cost more than the MAX monorail, buses, or Strip trolleys before you even start your journey, but they will always be faster and more convenient.

Rental cars can be booked at the same time you arrange your travel plans. If you are already in Las Vegas, the easiest way to hire a car is through your hotel. There are also many rental depots at the airport, but you can face long queues regardless of any previous booking. If your stay is only in Las Vegas, a rental car is not necessary. The Strip is often so clogged with traffic that it is easier to walk or use the monorail system. Taxi drivers know all the back entrances to all the hotels to

avoid congestion, and unless you know the same routes, a car may not be worth the expense.

Downtown, the Fremont Street area is pedestrianised and safe for tourists, but it is not recommended that you stray too far from these streets, particularly at night. A Downtown trolley runs from the Downtown Transportation Center on Stewart Avenue and Casino Center Boulevard every 30 minutes with stops that include Fremont Street.

There are many city-wide attractions beyond the Strip and the Downtown area, but even some hotel attractions are easy to miss – the establishments are so vast that you can get completely lost within rows of slot machines and gaming tables before you reach them.

Most hotels have booking desks for excursions and tourist information. Trips to the Hoover Dam or Grand Canyon are plentiful, and whether you want to see these sights by helicopter, plane or coach, transfers can be arranged from your hotel. Many museums and attractions in the city offer complimentary shuttle-bus services, which will collect you from your hotel if you call ahead.

As you walk along the Strip you will also be offered trips to the Hoover Dam or the Grand Canyon from the street, but although they may be sold by reputable companies, it is advisable to book trips through your hotel or travel agent, or even before you arrive.

History

1829   Las Vegas ('the meadows') is discovered by Spanish explorers.

1855   The area is settled by William Bringhurst and fellow Mormons.

1905   The Las Vegas town site is founded by Senator William J Clark.

1906   The Hotel Nevada opens Downtown.

1926   The first commercial plane lands in Las Vegas.

1931   Construction begins on the Boulder Dam (later renamed the Hoover Dam). Building is completed in 1935. Gambling is legalised in Nevada and new divorce laws bring tourists in for 'quickie' divorces and wedding ceremonies.

1941   Thomas Hull's El Rancho opens as the first hotel on the Las Vegas Strip.

1942   The Little Church of the West, the first wedding chapel on the Strip, opens in the grounds of the Last Frontier.

1944   Liberace comes to Las Vegas to perform on a $750-a-week contract at the Last Frontier.

1946   Mobster Ben 'Bugsy' Siegel opens his Flamingo Hotel on the Strip.

1951   Vegas Vic, the mechanical waving cowboy, is erected outside the Pioneer Club Downtown as a welcome greeting for visitors.

1952   The Sahara Hotel is opened with 240 rooms, the sixth hotel on the Strip.

1955   The Riviera is opened, the Strip's first skyrise. The Moulin Rouge is opened on Bonanza Road and is the first desegregated casino in Las Vegas.

1957   The Tropicana opens.

1958   The Stardust opens, with a record 1,000 rooms.

1959   The Las Vegas Convention Center opens its doors

with the World Congress of Flight exhibition. Wayne Newton makes his first appearance on the Strip and remains a headliner today.

1960 The Rat Pack (Frank Sinatra, Dean Martin, Sammy Davis Jr, Joey Bishop and Peter Lawford) hold their legendary summit at the Sands Hotel.

1964 The Beatles perform at the Las Vegas Convention Center.

1966 The reclusive Howard Hughes arrives in Las Vegas, famed for buying out the mob and becoming the largest landowner in Nevada.
Caesars Palace, the first of the luxurious themed hotels, opens on the Las Vegas Strip.
Frank Sinatra marries Mia Farrow in Las Vegas.

1967 Elvis Presley marries Priscilla Beaulieu at the year-old Aladdin Hotel.

1969 Kirk Kerkorian opens the International Hotel on Paradise Road. It is the largest hotel in the world.

Elvis Presley makes his stage comeback at the International Hotel and breaks all box-office records for the city.

1972 Jay Sarno, developer of Caesars Palace, opens Circus Circus Hotel & Casino Resort.

1979 The oriental-themed Imperial Palace Hotel & Casino is opened.

1989 After a quiet period of development on the Strip, Steve Wynn opens the Mirage, which kick-starts a new era of resort building. Legendary illusionists Siegfried and Roy are signed to a five-year $57.5-million contract.

1993 The Egyptian-themed Luxor Hotel is opened. Steve Wynn opens his Caribbean adventure hotel Treasure Island.
MGM Grand Hotel and theme park is opened with a record 5,005 rooms.

1994 The first Skywalks are built on the Las Vegas Strip.

1995 Downtown is rejuvenated with the opening of the

$70-million Fremont Street Experience.
The first Hard Rock Hotel is opened on Paradise Road.

1996 The Stratosphere is opened as the tallest structure west of the Mississippi River. The Sands Hotel is demolished, and plans are announced to replace it with a breathtaking mega-resort, later unveiled as The Venetian, which opens in 1999. Tiger Woods wins the Las Vegas Invitational.

1997 New York-New York Hotel & Casino is opened, receiving over 100,000 visitors a day in its first few days on the Las Vegas Strip.

1998 Bellagio opens on the Las Vegas Strip, costing a record $1.6 billion, and features the largest choreographed water fountain in the world.

1999 The tropical-themed Mandalay Bay Resort opens on the site of the former Hacienda Hotel. The new resort includes a Four Seasons Hotel on the upper floors.

Paris Las Vegas opens on 1 September.

2000 In the largest corporate buyout in gaming history, Kirk Kerkorian's MGM Grand Inc. acquires Steve Wynn's Mirage Resorts, and in the following years MGM also plan to buy out the Mandalay Group.

2001 *Ocean's Eleven* is remade 41 years after the original Las Vegas heist was filmed by the Rat Pack in 1960.

2002 Neonopolis, an 18,580sq m (200,000sq ft) entertainment complex, opens at the *Fremont Street Experience* in Downtown Las Vegas.

2003 In a move away from family themed resorts, Treasure Island is transformed into TI, while the Las Vegas Convention and Visitors Authority create a new advertising slogan for the city with the tagline 'What Happens Here, Stays Here.' Another Vegas chapter ends when the Siegfried & Roy show closes after illusionist Roy Horn is mauled on stage by a tiger.

2004   Costing $654 million, the Las Vegas Monorail opens, running the full length of the Strip from the MGM Grand, at the southern end of Las Vegas Boulevard, to the Sahara Hotel.

2005   Steve Wynn exceeds his Bellagio price tag to open Wynn Las Vegas, the most expensive hotel in the world, at a cost of $2.7 billion, while Las Vegas celebrates its 100th birthday.

2006   Planet Hollywood Hotel & Casino opens on the site of the 40-year-old Aladdin Hotel. Caesars Palace plans a $1 billion expansion and renovation.

2007   The development company Las Vegas Sands opens the multi-billion resort Palazzo. Hotel construction in this year exceeds $4 billion, resulting in over 4,000 new hotel rooms and an additional 44,500sq m (480,000sq ft) of convention space.

2008   Celebrity chef Charlie Palmer begins construction of a luxury condo-hotel that introduces a non-gambling dimension to Downtown, with an emphasis on intimacy and pampering. Frank Gehry's stunning metal lattice structure opens in Union Park as the Alzheimer's Research Center, a 'Museum of the Mind'.

2009   Resort owner Steve Wynn opens the $2.1 billion Encore, adjacent to Wynn Las Vegas, featuring a 6,875sq m (74,000sq ft) casino. MGM's CityCenter breaks the record for the most expensive hotel complex in the world as the 27-hectare (67-acre) resort is unveiled at a cost of $9.2 billion.

2010   Despite the recession and the postponement of some big Vegas hotel developments, the city continues to renew itself with the Harmon Hotel & Spa due to open in the CityCenter development with 400 new rooms, as well as the Cosmopolitan Resort on the Strip with almost 3,000 rooms.

Helldorado

Contrary to Hollywood legend, Las Vegas welcomed gamblers, gangsters and Hollywood celebrities long before Ben 'Bugsy' Siegel swung open the doors of his Flamingo Hotel & Casino in 1946. This notorious wiseguy is often credited as the founding father of Las Vegas, but he was certainly not the first to break ground in the oasis.

The desert area known as Las Vegas, or 'the meadows', was originally discovered in 1829, located just off the old Spanish trail from New Mexico to California, which had been frequented by travellers and explorers since the 1700s. The first detailed maps of the area were created by Captain John C Frémont, who described two warm springs in his journal, writing: 'The taste of the water is good, but rather too warm to be agreeable; the temperature being 71 in one and 73 in the other. They, however, afforded a delightful bathing place.'

The area was later home to a small Mormon community, but without the luxury of air conditioning the missionaries were unable to withstand the desert temperatures. The Mormons left within two years, leaving behind an abandoned fort, which is still preserved today as a state historic park.

The city was officially founded in May 1905, during a historic auction in which railroad tycoon William J Clark sold lots on his new Las Vegas town site. A year later the Hotel Nevada was opened Downtown and still

Ben 'Bugsy' Siegel's Flamingo Hotel & Casino

stands today as the Golden Gate Hotel and Casino.

Although drinking and gambling were both prohibited in the early 20th century, visitors and residents frequented Block 16, an area designated by Clark's railroad company for the consumption of liquor. Prohibition laws were also ignored to celebrate the construction of the Boulder Dam, which brought a promise of work to an economy crippled by the Great Depression.

In 1931 gambling was legalised throughout Nevada. As state officials had already closed down Block 16, in the fear that it was corrupting Las Vegas residents, legitimate casino owners began developing new establishments two blocks away around Fremont and Second Street. The Apache and El Cortez were some of the first to appear during an unprecedented neon boom, which created the Downtown area known for its gaudy façades and sparkling illuminations, as Glitter Gulch.

Starting in 1935, this new city was appropriately promoted with Helldorado, a yearly festival that featured a street rodeo, competitions and carnival parade. But new developments outside town changed the city landscape forever.

According to legend, Thomas Hull, a hotel owner from California, visited Las Vegas in the late 1930s to look

The luxurious Mandalay Bay and Four Seasons Hotel now stand on the site of the former Hacienda

for new property. His car overheated a few kilometres south of the city and, amazed by the volume of traffic heading downtown, he decided to build his hotel outside the city limits. Thomas Hull's El Rancho opened in 1941 and became the first hotel on the Las Vegas Strip. It was followed a year later by the Last Frontier, but was shortly eclipsed by the Flamingo, a lavish development that ushered in the future of glittering, conspicuous resorts. These included the Hacienda, which set up its own Hacienda Airlines to fly customers into Vegas. These glamorous resorts have evolved over a period of 50 years to become the Las Vegas of today – luxurious hotels within a paradise for all ages.

Politics

Residents of California can elect actors and action heroes such as Arnold Schwarzenegger as State Governor. But only in Las Vegas could they elect a former Mafia attorney as Mayor.

In its brief history, Las Vegas has been governed by several factions – from the gun laws of the Old West, to Mafia mob rule and corruption in its early days as a tourist attraction, to the corporate ownership that dominates the city today.

When the city was founded in the early 20th century, residents had little regard for the law or those that enforced it upon them, and the same men that provided the rail lines or city resources, such as water and electricity, also controlled politics. Although drinking and gambling were prohibited at the beginning of the century, county officials and politicians seemed to be immune from prosecution and joined the residents in Downtown Block 16, where a blind eye was turned to their indulgence in drinking, gambling and prostitution.

An early Justice of the Peace was a blacksmith named Jacob Ralph, who would use his business premises as a courtroom. The fine for any misdemeanour usually equated to the amount of money the accused held in his pocket when he was brought before the judge.

The city's second Sheriff, Sam Gay, stands out as a lawman with greater principles. This broad six-footer did not touch alcohol and could break up any fight without drawing a gun, as he preferred to grab the wrongdoers by the scruff of their necks and knock their heads together, then save his target practice for the twinkling new lights in the city.

Today, with almost $9 billion gained in county gaming revenue, locals claim it is the casinos that call the shots. On average, Las Vegas casinos pay half the amount in taxes that the rest of the country has to surrender, while extra taxes are levied on small businesses and entertainment. The Federal Government is often called to investigate bribes allegedly taken by councillors and commissioners from establishments such as strip clubs, while locals claim that the best lawmen they ever had in town were the Mafia.

Throughout the 1940s and '50s, glamorous new resorts began appearing on the Las Vegas Strip. The Flamingo, the Sands, the Desert Inn, the Tropicana, the Thunderbird, the Sahara, the Stardust, the Dunes and the Riviera may have looked like legitimate businesses, but the real ownership and control of these establishments was exerted by Mafia families spread across the whole of the United States.

Surprisingly, the mob was often an attraction for Las Vegas visitors, but during the 1960s government officials began a determined campaign to crack down on organised crime, which started a new era in corporate ownership in the city.

While an aggressive tourism campaign has almost erased the city's unfavourable history, city Mayor Oscar Goodman wants to revive the ghosts of his wiseguy buddies. The city council has approved plans to open a Downtown mob exhibit – where the Mafia's very own defence lawyer can finally pay homage to the men who gave him 'juice' in the city.

The Federal Courthouse has seen its share of mob defendants

Culture

Las Vegas has its own unique culture. In the 1930s and '40s, as the new city grew, it clung to its roots in the Old West. The population boomed with job seekers keen to escape the dust-bowl states as hopeful workers signed up for construction of the Boulder Dam. The new gambling laws brought in speculators and entrepreneurs, and entertainers soon joined the throng, creating a city with a wide cultural diversity.

Native Americans were the first settlers in southern Nevada, followed by Spanish explorers, who were the first Europeans to reach the area, in the early 1800s. The Hispanic influence can be seen today in landscaping, art and architecture but is most evident in the city's name (Spanish for 'the meadows'). The French and British followed the Spanish and were soon accompanied by a huge mix of European settlers. Asian and Pacific Islanders began their migration to the area in the 1800s, working as miners, ranchers or labourers, particularly on the expanding railroads. While Europe was threatened by Nazi Germany, Jewish settlers were not victimised in Nevada and their businesses flourished; throughout the 1940s and '50s many of the new Strip establishments were owned by Jewish investors.

Many African-American entertainers such as Sammy Davis Jr and Nat King Cole performed on the Strip from its early days, but while the Civil Rights movement made great headway in the rest of the country, Las Vegas was slow to respond. To black entertainers in the 1950s, the city was known as the

Culture Las Vegas style at The Venetian resort

The *Fiore di Como* by Dale Chihully decorates the ceiling of the Bellagio lobby

'Mississippi of the West'. While they could perform on the Strip, they were not welcome offstage, regardless of how famous they were. As glamorous high-rise hotels grew in the city, a small motel on Bonanza Road changed history when in 1955 the Moulin Rouge became the first desegregated casino in Las Vegas.

Today, Las Vegas is a huge melting pot of cultures and nationalities, expressed in hotels with all-American themes such as New York-New York, in the European-influenced Paris, Venetian and Bellagio, and in the oriental-themed Imperial Palace. Cuisine is offered by award-winning chefs from across the globe, while world-famous entertainers and performers, from Tom Jones to Prince

and Elton John, grace the stages. In 1993 the Cirque du Soleil, a production company that employs talented individuals from over 40 different countries, made its Las Vegas debut with *Mystère*. German-born illusionists Siegfried & Roy were headliners on the Strip, while the famous showgirl revues such as *Folies Bergère* and *La Femme* originated in Paris. In 2000 the critically acclaimed Blue Man Group opened at the Luxor Hotel and defied description with its multimedia, sensory-blurring performance art.

World-famous works of art are displayed in the Bellagio Gallery of Fine Art, while at Wynn Las Vegas the owner Steve Wynn puts paintings by artists such as Picasso and Rembrandt on display in the public areas of the hotel.

Viva Las Vegas

Las Vegas is famed for its opulent hotel properties, every form of gambling from penny slots to high stakes baccarat, beautiful showgirls, mysterious illusionists and stunning production shows and headliners, all combining to earn the desert city its title as entertainment capital of the world.

Everybody who is anybody has played Las Vegas: Frank Sinatra and his Rat Pack, Elvis Presley, Liberace, the Beatles, the Stones, the Three Tenors, Tom Jones and Celine Dion have all headlined in the city, along with many others too numerous to name here. Alongside the celebrities, hotels have their own shows, comedy clubs, live music venues, sporting events and convention centres.

The most celebrated productions in Las Vegas are presented by the world-class Cirque du Soleil. Formed in 1984, its shows have been seen by an audience of over 90 million across the globe and feature a cast from 40 countries. Cirque du Soleil always has several shows resident in Las Vegas, such as *Mystère*, '*O*' and *Zumanity*.

Mystère opened in Treasure Island (now known as TI) in 1993 and has been named the Best Production Show in Las Vegas on numerous occasions. With world-class acrobats, gymnasts and musicians along with high aerial ballets and stunts, *Mystère* is described as the journey of human potential.

In phonetic terms, '*O*' is French for *eau* or water. Showing at the Bellagio, each scene takes place in, on or above water, as the stage is set around a pool of water measuring 30 by 45m (100 by 150ft) and 7.5m (25ft) deep. Performers include trapeze artists, divers and synchronised swimmers in a spectacular piece of theatre, which has also been named Best Production Show in Las Vegas.

The imposing MGM Grand, home to the Arena venue

Caesars Palace has brought headliners to the Strip since 1966

Resident in New York-New York, *Zumanity – Another Side of Cirque Du Soleil* has been described as risqué, sensual and alluring, with some very erotic scenes, yet demonstrates the remarkable capabilities of the human body.

In February 2005, Cirque du Soleil premiered *KÀ* at the MGM Grand, which presents an epic tale of two imperial twins. The show features an impressive cast of 80 performers, with outstanding martial arts, acrobatics, puppetry and a dazzling display of special effects and pyrotechnics.

In 2006 Cirque du Soleil opened the new show *Love* at the Mirage. Showcasing the music of the Beatles, it uses a special soundtrack prepared at Abbey Road Studios in London. Then in 2010 another great music legend, Mr Las Vegas himself, Elvis Presley, got the Cirque du Soleil treatment when they premiered *Viva ELVIS* at the new ARIA Resort and Casino in the CityCenter.

Caesars Palace added the 4,000-seat, $95-million Colosseum to its property where headliners include Céline Dion in *A New Day*, which is produced by Cirque du Soleil's Franco Dragone, and Elton John in his acclaimed show *The Red Piano*.

Along with Steve Wynn, Franco Dragone is also the creator of *Le Rêve*, a stunning new production with over 70 world-class performers, featuring a 3.8-million-litre (836,000-gallon) pool surrounded by 2,080 seats all at centre stage.

Las Vegas is also home to huge event centres such as the MGM Grand Arena and the Mandalay Bay Events Center. Added to the city's ever-growing list of showrooms and theatres, the choice for entertainment is truly endless.

Festivals and events

As well as being a tourist destination, Las Vegas attracts 4.5 million convention delegates each year, along with sports fans who come for golf championships, boxing matches, basketball games and several rodeo events. Since the first resorts began appearing on the Strip in the 1940s, music fans have chosen Las Vegas as the destination to see their favourite singing stars, and the city also plays host to ceremonies such as the Billboard Music Awards.

January

In January 150 drivers compete in the **Laughlin Desert Challenge**, where desert race cars and trucks race from sunrise to sunset in a SCORE International off-road racing event.

February

If Fremont Street is not lively enough, in February it plays host to the **Las Vegas Mardi Gras**. Other city events include the **Las Vegas International Marathon** and the **Big League Challenge**.

March

Eight men's and women's basketball teams compete in 14 games for the **Mountain West Conference Basketball Championship**, while the Las Vegas Motor Speedway is host to the **Shelby American** and the **Sam's Town 300 NASCAR**. Top cowboys compete in the **Laughlin Rodeo Days**, which include the **Laughlin River Stampede PRCA Rodeo**, where cowboys attempt to win over $225,000 in prize money.

April

Baseball fans meet in Las Vegas for the **Big League Weekend** just before the start of the season. The **Laughlin River Run** welcomes over 50,000 bikers, who gather for five days for the largest Harley-Davidson motorcycle rally in the West.

May

Las Vegas is the final destination for the **EA SPORTS Supercross Series**, the last of 16 events around the US. The Las Vegas meeting attracts 40,000 spectators to the Sam Boyd Stadium.

June

Film fans normally flock to the city for the **CineVegas International**, but the 2010 event was suspended due to the recession; it is still uncertain whether the 2011 festival will take place.

September

Top bull riders from the Professional Bull Riders Bud Light Cup tour compete for the $100,000 prize money in the **Laughlin Shoot Out**. The city presents the **Las Vegas Stampede**, while the Primm **300 SCORE International** race takes place on the California–Nevada border.

October

The Las Vegas Motor Speedway plays host to **Las Vegas Bike Week**, the **AMA Superbike Championships**, the **NASCAR Craftsman Truck Series Race** and the **World of Outlaws/NASCAR Winston West Races**. The **Justin Timberlake Shriners Hospitals for Children Open** sees PGA Tour golfers competing in Las Vegas, while the longest hitters play the **Re/Max World Long Drive Championships** in Mesquite.

November

The **PDR Bud Light World Championships** in Las Vegas see the top 45 bull riders compete for $1.5-million in prize money. The best ropers take part in the **Laughlin Team Roping**, while **Wendy's Three-Tour Challenge** invites teams from the PGA Tour, Senior PGA Tour and LPGA Tour to take part.

December

The **PRCA's National Finals Rodeo**, the World Series of rodeos, returns to Las Vegas for a ten-day stint, while the **Billboard Music Awards** take place at the MGM Grand Garden Arena. NCAA (National Collegiate Athletic Association) basketball players compete in the **Las Vegas Showdown**, while the **Sega Sports Las Vegas Bowl** takes place at the Sam Boyd Stadium at UNLV, featuring the second selection from the Mountain West Conference and the fifth selection from the Pac-10 Conference. Finally, the year ends with the city's sensational fireworks spectacular along the Strip.

The enormous Las Vegas Convention Center, home to many of the city's events

Impressions

It may have been captured in countless Hollywood blockbusters, but even the big screen cannot do Las Vegas justice. This sparkling entity is also impossible to convey in a guidebook. You cannot communicate the unique sights and sounds, or the feel of the warm desert sun within a few pages – Las Vegas is the ultimate must-see destination.

Before you leave

Before you book any flights or make any other travel arrangements, make sure there are hotel rooms available on the dates you wish to visit. Over 80 per cent of the hotel rooms are booked during the week, while the occupancy runs at over 90 per cent at the weekends. This is greatly affected by public holidays such as Thanksgiving or Labor Day, and when special events or festivals are taking place. Las Vegas also welcomes 4.5 million convention delegates every year, and at times the impact of all these visitors means that there are few rooms available and you could end up paying a room price many times higher than the usual rate.

Roller coaster at New York-New York

If you choose to book through a travel agent, or you are travelling as part of a tour, the fixed price you pay will be based on the season and will allow for fluctuations due to other events.

How to get there

Las Vegas is located at the southern tip of Nevada and is serviced by McCarran International Airport, located just south of the Strip. The airport manages over 44 million passengers each year, connecting it with most locations within the United States. If you are flying in from overseas, only a few airlines offer direct flights, as most carriers will fly you to a gateway city first.

By car, Las Vegas is 469km (291 miles) east of Los Angeles on Interstate 15, nestled between the California and Arizona borders, and on the Reno-to-Phoenix Interstate 95. From the west coast it's a long desert drive that will take between four and five hours, so make sure your vehicle is roadworthy for the journey and keep an eye on fuel consumption. Bear in mind that the air conditioning in your car will also affect your petrol usage, and for most of the year you will be unable to make this journey without it.

When to visit Las Vegas

Las Vegas is a year-round 24-hour city. To avoid the crowds, plan your visit away from public holidays, and try to visit during weekdays (Sunday to Thursday). The only days that

The celebrity favourite – the Palms hotel

attractions may be closed are Christmas Day and possibly Thanksgiving.

Las Vegas is warm all year round, but during the summer months between June and the end of August temperatures can reach well over 38°C (100°F). Peak season runs from April to September, and the best time to visit is at the start or tail end of the season, when Las Vegas will still be very warm. In winter, out of the sunlight or during the evening, there is a marked drop in temperature.

What to wear

The most important item to pack is a pair of comfortable shoes. The Las Vegas Strip is over 5km (3 miles) long, and you will cover vast distances just by visiting the hotels and their attractions. Even if you cover only a third of the Strip, you can get lost in each hotel

There are several walkways where you can cross the Strip

for hours. The dress code is casual in Las Vegas. In the summer, take shorts, T-shirts and light comfortable clothing. It is advisable to protect your skin from the sun, but ensure you apply a high-factor sun cream for any exposed areas. In winter, it's a good idea to pack a jacket or warmer clothes, particularly for the evening.

A few restaurants and shows have a formal dress code, so pack something for those occasions. There are many new nightclubs in Las Vegas, and some of these have relaxed dress codes (and admission fees) for women, but stricter rules for men, who may not be allowed in if wearing trainers or jeans.

Arriving in Las Vegas

If you arrive by air, try to book your flight to arrive in the evening, so you can get your first glimpse of Las Vegas by night. The city appears so large and luminous you feel as if you are landing right next to the Strip. In true Vegas style, the inside of the airport is filled with fruit machines. If you arrive between Thursday and Saturday, expect the airport to be busy, particularly in the baggage-claim area.

At the time of booking your trip or accommodation, you may be offered transport to your hotel: this will be located just outside the baggage claim, along with taxis and limousine services. One of the easiest and most cost-effective ways to reach your hotel is to purchase a shuttle-bus ticket from one of the many booths in this area, which can take you to any of the Strip or Downtown hotels. Most of these buses offer a return ticket, and you will have to ring and reserve a pick-up shuttle the day before you intend to leave. After a long journey, many flustered passengers easily lose their return tickets for this service, so keep them somewhere safe, preferably with your travel documents.

Tipping

From the moment you arrive in Las Vegas – or anywhere in the United States – you will realise that every good service requires a tip. Expect to add 15–20 per cent to your restaurant bill, and unless seating is assigned, pay showroom maitre d's $5–20 for a good seat. Cocktail waitresses expect $1–2 per round, and 15 per cent of the journey fare should be given to taxi drivers. The valet that beckons your cab will also expect a tip for his efforts. $2–5 per day should be paid for housekeeping on departure, and a similar gratuity should also be paid to tour guides, for valet parking and for each piece of luggage carried by a hotel porter.

If you are playing card games, roulette or craps, it is good gaming etiquette to tip the croupier if you have a run of good luck, or to place a bet on their behalf. Card dealers, slot attendants and keno runners should also receive a gratuity.

European splendour at the Monte Carlo Resort and Casino

Ten of the best

Las Vegas is sure to keep you busy, whether you come to gamble or to sample some of the city's other offerings. Here are ten highlights that you should check out.

The *Fountains of Bellagio*
On its grand opening in 1998, the Bellagio was credited as the most expensive hotel ever built. The hotel is based upon an Italian village of the same name and is set around a 3.4-hectare (8.5-acre) lake, featuring the largest musical fountain display in the world. *See p38*.

The Strip at night
You can't beat a long walk along the Strip when the sun has gone down and the neon lights have come on. It's a spectacular sight, and thrilling no matter how many times you've been to Vegas before.

The Forum Shops at Caesars
In the luxurious setting of Caesars Palace, the Forum Shops contain over 65,000sq m (700,000sq ft) of retail space. As well as an overwhelming selection of more than 160 shops, consumer heaven is famed for its talking Roman statues and breathtaking architecture. *See p158*.

The *Fremont Street Experience*
Live music, street entertainers and a laser show cover a four-block section of Downtown Las Vegas. A canopy above the street features 12.5 million LED lamps to create a free animated performance on the largest screen of its kind in the world. *See pp74–5*.

The Grand Canyon
This awe-inspiring natural wonder is 445km (277 miles) long and up to 16km (10 miles) wide and 1.6km (1 mile) deep. There are visitor centres on the north and south rims of the canyon as well as many scenic viewpoints. Several tours operate from Las Vegas and the easiest way to see the canyon is by plane or helicopter. *See pp114–19*.

The Hoover Dam
Proclaimed by President Hoover as 'a 20th-century marvel', the Hoover Dam is one of the greatest achievements in the industrial world. Completed in 1935, the Dam restrains the unpredictable Colorado River to meet domestic water needs and provide low-cost hydroelectric power for residents of Nevada, California and Arizona. *See pp122–3*.

New York-New York

For exciting themed architecture and streetscapes, look no further than New York-New York. The exterior resembles the Manhattan skyline, complete with skyscrapers, the Brooklyn Bridge and the Statue of Liberty among other key buildings, while the interior is based around the city streets. *See pp34–5.*

Cirque du Soleil

The original production entitled *Mystère* at Treasure Island features 72 dancers, acrobats, musicians and singers entwined in a mesmerising display of human athleticism, agility and energy. At the Bellagio, theatre enters a whole new realm with 'O', Cirque du Soleil's aquatic production, which is a sensational and innovative homage to musical genres from humble street artists to operatic extravaganzas. At the new Aria Resort in the CityCenter, the group's latest production is *Viva ELVIS*, a tribute to the King of Rock 'n' Roll from these kings and queens of dramatic acrobatics. *See pp20–21.*

The Stratosphere

For the best view of Las Vegas and the wildest and highest thrill rides in the city, visit the Stratosphere Tower. You cannot miss this 350m (1,149ft) space needle at the north end of the Strip. *See pp46 & 55–6.*

Wynn Las Vegas

Everything you could expect, and more, from acclaimed resort developer Steve Wynn. Where lakes, fountains, waterfalls and lagoons meet the ultimate luxury that comes with a $2.7 billion price tag. The Wynn also boasts the **Penske–Wynn Ferrari–Maserati** showroom with some vehicles costing in excess of $1 million. *See pp51, 53 & 54–5.*

The luxurious Wynn Las Vegas opened in 2005

The Las Vegas Strip

As you drive in from Los Angeles, or travel on Highway 91 from McCarran International airport, you are greeted by the old familiar sign, 'Welcome to Las Vegas'. This is the southern tip of the Las Vegas Strip.

The best way to see the Strip is on foot. Stunning as these resorts appear from the outside, just wait until you see the inside. You do not have to be a hotel resident to enter.

As you head north, the sparkling vision of gold before you is the Mandalay Bay resort and casino, radiant and imposing, and this is just the beginning. As you drive up between the palm trees you will pass the striking black pyramid of the Luxor, guarded by its huge Egyptian sphinx, the skyline of Manhattan and the Statue of Liberty at New York-New York, then the domineering MGM Grand, Monte Carlo and Planet Hollywood.

With its bright lights, the Las Vegas Strip is an incredible sight. By night, the neon blazes and twinkles, but by day, under a sapphire-blue desert sky, the resorts are even more colourful while the neon still glistens under the sun.

Heading up the Strip you see the sumptuous Bellagio, with its magnificent lake and fountain display, and across the street Paris, complete with its Eiffel Tower. Beyond this is the legendary Caesars Palace, an affluent resort fronted by Roman statues, fountains, a colosseum and landscaped gardens. After a little ancient history you have a taste of Las Vegas ancestry with the Flamingo Hotel, the first luxurious resort in a town once steeped in the Old West.

Another beautiful European city is depicted in The Venetian, which stands opposite the exotic paradise Mirage, with its erupting volcano, and TI, or Treasure Island, home of the controversial TV show *The Sirens of TI*.

Las Vegas is always evolving, and dream resorts such as the Wynn and Encore have replaced grand old dames such as the New Frontier and Stardust. At the north end of the Strip the Echelon Resort will eventually reign supreme on the site where the Stardust long embodied the fabulous '50s. Originally scheduled for 2010, the Echelon has been delayed because of the recession. With a new burst of radiance from the Sahara, the grand finale on the Strip is the Stratosphere tower, the tallest building west of the Mississippi.

Ladies and gentlemen – welcome to Las Vegas.

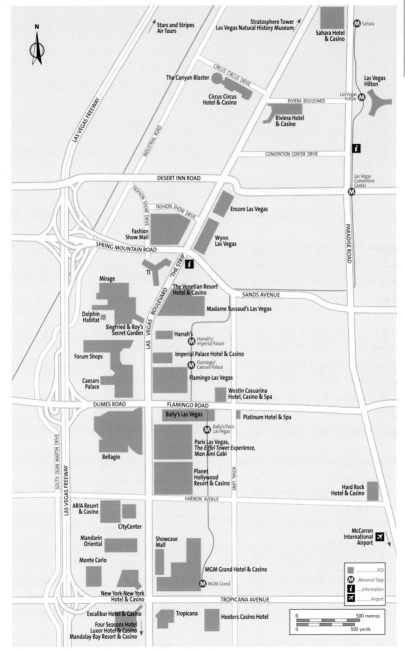

Mandalay Bay

The Mandalay Bay complex incorporates three distinct hotels, each with its own entrance and style, although they're usually referred to collectively by the name of the original: Mandalay Bay. But here too are the Four Seasons-Las Vegas and the suites-only THEhotel. Mandalay Bay went up in 1999, adding a South Seas theme to the Las Vegas Strip, a theme which still pervades the resort even where some other Vegas hotels are down-playing their own identities. And with a massive 4.5 hectares (11 acres) of beach within the property, you could indeed be in some South Sea island escape at times.

As well as the Beach (as it's called), there's a wave pool, a lazy river, waterfalls, grottoes and lagoons. There's the Beachside Casino, which is spread over three floors and where you can gamble in the open air without changing out of your swimming gear. Also here at the Beach is night-time entertainment at the House of Blues Music Hall, which has featured headline acts like Joss Stone, Blondie, Boz Scaggs, Jimmy Cliff, the Wailers and Ziggy Marley. If you're not into lounging by the pool, Mandalay Bay has 18 restaurants (inlcuding one by Charlie Palmer), 9 bars, a gym, the Bathhouse Spa and a tropical-themed casino.

For entertainment, as well as the House of Blues Music Hall, the resort has Disney's *The Lion King* on one of its stages, and a 12,000-seat arena, which hosts major sporting events like boxing, as well as music concerts from big names on tour.

Shark Reef Aquarium

One of the hotel's big attractions, which appeals to children as well as adults, is Shark Reef Aquarium. North America's sole predator-based aquarium is a unique aquatic experience, home to many exotic and dangerous species. Visitors receive a passport-style guide with un facts, maps and guidelines, as well as a hand-held audio device that explains all of the animals and fish on display.

As you enter Shark Reef, you encounter the golden crocodiles. A hybrid of Siamese and saltwater crocodiles, these are the only examples of this reptile outside Thailand. They may seem harmless as they float sedately on the top of the water, but these are ferocious predators and it would take four men to restrain each one.

The aquarium also features two glass walkthroughs, the Front Reef Tunnel and Back Reef Tunnel, which contain coral reefs populated with vibrant fish such as the stars and stripes puffer, the purple tang and the Picasso trigger. Dominating these tunnels, majestic sharks soar over your head and around the tanks at great speed, and include the zebra, bonnethead and black tip reef shark. The most impressive display of sea life can be seen around the sunken pirate ship, which is populated by more than 40 different sharks. Housed in 5 million litres (just over 1 million gallons) of water, these predators are joined by sea turtles, moray eels, stingrays and several other species of fish. Sharks in this tank include the lemon shark, one of the most dangerous sharks in the world, as well as the fearsome-looking sand tiger shark.

Open: Sun–Thur 10am–8pm, Fri & Sat 10am–10pm (last admission 1 hour before closing). Admission charge.

www.mandalaybay.com (see p133).

(see p133)

A majestic stingray at Shark Reef Aquarium

The Las Vegas Strip

New York-New York

The exterior of New York-New York Hotel and Casino is certainly the most impressive display of architecture on the Las Vegas Strip. Designed to re-create the Manhattan skyline, New York-New York is fronted by a 45m (150ft) replica of the Statue of Liberty surrounded by a stunning display of city landscapes, including hotel guestrooms located in twelve Manhattan skyscrapers featuring the Empire State Building, the Chrysler Building and the New Yorker Hotel among others.

At the foot of the Statue of Liberty there is a 90m (300ft) replica of the Brooklyn Bridge, added to many other features, including Grand Central Station and Ellis Island immigration terminal. Following the terrorist attacks on the World Trade Center in 2001, a September 11 tribute was added to the base of the statue when items were placed there in remembrance of those lost in the rescue services.

The final touch is the Manhattan Express roller coaster, which races around the exterior of the structure and back inside to the Coney Island Emporium. The interior of the hotel is equally impressive, with a 7,800sq m (84,000sq ft) casino surrounded by the streets of New York, complete with lampposts and manholes that emit steam. Replica areas include Park Avenue, New York's Financial District, Times Square, Central Park and a Greenwich Village neighbourhood with several shopfronts, bars, cafés and restaurants along the sidewalks.

Within New York-New York you can eat at Nine Fine Irishmen, Gallagher's Steakhouse, Il Fornaio, ESPN Zone, Chin Chin Café, Gonzalez y Gonzalez, America, Nathan's and Quick Bites.

Entertainment New York style includes Coyote Ugly, a saloon bar based on the movie of the same name, the Center Bar and the Bar at Times Square, with its live duelling pianos. New York-New York's headline attraction is *Zumanity*, an erotic production, described as both edgy and provocative, created by the celebrated Cirque du Soleil.
www.nynyhotelcasino.com (see p132).

MANHATTAN SKYLINE

New York-New York's Manhattan Skyline is re-created with towers that are approximately one-third the height of the actual city skyscrapers.

The Empire State Building: 161m (529ft), 47 storeys

The Century Building: 127m (416ft), 41 storeys

The Seagram Building: 91m (300ft), 30 storeys

The 55 Water Tower: 36 storeys

The Lever House Soap Company: 29 storeys

The Municipal Building: 29 storeys, plus a 24m (80ft) tower

The AT&T Building: 26 storeys

The Chrysler Building: 152m (500ft), 40 storeys

The CBS Building: 29 storeys

The New Yorker Hotel: 113m (370ft), 34 storeys

The Liberty Plaza: 31 storeys

The Ziggurat Building: 38 storeys

Fronted by the Statue of Liberty, New York-New York is a celebrated example of Las Vegas architecture

Tour: The Mafia

From the 1940s, crime families from all over the USA invested heavily in the Las Vegas Strip. No wonder that it is known as the city the mob built. By the end of the 1970s their reign was over, but these wiseguys created a legend that continues to inspire moviemakers, fascinate historians and add glamour to the tourist trade.

Allow one day. Use the Las Vegas monorail to reach some resorts.

1 The Tropicana

In 1959, Frank Costello survived an assassination attempt. The bullet that was meant to kill the Prime Minister of the Underworld only grazed his skull but rendered him unconscious. When the police searched his pockets they found the first hard evidence of the Mafia's stranglehold on Las Vegas: a record of the day's takings at the Tropicana.

In December 2010, the Las Vegas Mob Experience opens at the Tropicana. It will be an interactive experience in which some of the legendary gangsters will appear and give first-person accounts of what it was like to be part of the world of organised crime. Accompanying this will be the largest collection of authentic personal items, videos, photos and other artefacts ever seen together in the same place.
Head north along the Strip until you are past the junction with Flamingo Road.

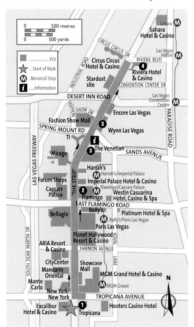

2 The Flamingo

Bugsy Siegel's dream resort was opened in 1946, but with construction

Frank Costello controlled a huge gambling empire

costs in excess of $6 million, he repaid that debt with his life. The Flamingo was the third hotel on the Strip, but the first of many mob-owned establishments that would appear over the next few years. Enjoy a cocktail in Bugsy's Bar located inside the Flamingo and open 24 hours a day.
Continue north. Your next stops are either side of Sands Avenue.

3 The Venetian and Wynn Las Vegas

Now The Venetian, the Sands Hotel was owned by a mob collective that included Meyer Lansky, Joe Adonis, Frank Costello and singer Frank Sinatra, who had a nine per cent stake in the resort. Wynn stands on the site of the Desert Inn, originally owned by Moe Dalitz and the Cleveland Mob. The hotel featured in the first two *Godfather* movies as a Corleone family investment.

Continue north along the Strip until you reach Convention Center Drive. You will see the site of the famous Stardust Hotel & Casino on the left side of the Strip (it was demolished in 2007). It was originally developed in 1958 by Tony Cornero, who mainly operated on the wrong side of the law managing offshore casino boats and profiteering from the prohibition era when he kept the liquor flowing in Las Vegas saloons. After his death, the Stardust soon became a goldmine for the mob, who skimmed huge profits. Its colourful history was dramatised in the film Casino. *Go a little further north and cross the road.*

4 Riviera Hotel & Casino

Chicago bosses such as Sam Giancana once owned the Riviera, and two of the Marx Brothers also invested in the hotel when it opened in 1955.
Open: Tue–Sat 5.30–10.30pm.
Retrace your steps back down the Strip.

Bellagio

The magnificent Bellagio hotel is the essence of Las Vegas opulence and style. Based on the northern Italian village of the same name, its grand opening took place in October 1998. At the base of the resort, surrounding the lake, is a collection of bars and restaurants, designed to re-create village properties found around the hotel's namesake on Lake Como.

There are moving walkways, and side entrances from Caesars Palace and through the Via Bellagio shops. Once inside the hotel, its $1.6-billion price tag is more than evident. One stunning feature is the ceiling of the hotel lobby, the *Fiore di Como*, with over 2,000 suspended glass flowers, each one unique, before casting your eyes down to the breathtaking marble walkways that guide you through the casino and out towards the Bellagio Conservatory and Botanical Gardens. Here, you'll be presented with an impressive display of flora in keeping with the current season or major holidays.

In the same area you will often see a queue forming for the popular Buffet at Bellagio, and you will be impressed by the sweeping staircases leading towards the spa and wedding chapels.

Bellagio has many casual and fine-dining restaurants throughout the property, although some of its lakeside establishments may not be within everyone's price range. Hotel restaurants include the 24-hour Café Bellagio, the Petrossian Bar and the Buffet at Bellagio, or you can sample award-winning pastries at Jean-Philippe Patisserie or enjoy cocktail hour at the Caramel Bar and Lounge. The resort offers a world of cuisine with ten dining options, including Italian food at Circo, Chinese at Jasmine, Michelin-starred chef Michael Mina, French dining at the award-winning Le Cirque and Picasso, and poolside dining at the Pool Café.

Bellagio is home to the Cirque du Soleil's acclaimed production 'O', with a cast of 81 artists performing in, on and above a 5.7-million-litre (1.2-million-gallon) pool of water. The Mediterranean pool area offers five pools with hand-carved stone fountains and spas.

THE *FOUNTAINS OF BELLAGIO*

One of the most spectacular free shows on the Las Vegas Strip is the choreographed display *Fountains of Bellagio*. Dancing streams of water are created by water-emitting devices, called oarsmen, in addition to mini-shooters and super-shooters that can reach a height of 72m (240ft). Over 1,000 fountains span more than 300m (1,000ft) across Lake Bellagio to create the largest musical fountain system in the world. The displays are choreographed to music ranging from Luciano Pavarotti and Andrea Bocelli to Gene Kelly, Frank Sinatra and Lionel Richie. The display can be seen from both sides of the Strip, but if the sidewalk is too crowded with onlookers, the bridge that connects Bellagio with Bally's offers a good vantage point.
Free shows: Mon–Fri 3pm–midnight, Sat & Sun midday–midnight. Every 30 minutes until 8pm, then every 15 minutes.

You must be at least 18 years of age to enter the Bellagio unless you are staying there.

Bellagio Gallery of Fine Art

The Bellagio is also famed for its art gallery. When developer and art collector Steve Wynn opened it in 1998, the city was suddenly recognised as a centre for the visual arts where you could view revered masterpieces and see the very best contemporary work from local, national and international artists. The gallery presents museum-calibre exhibitions from many prestigious international collections. Recent exhibitions have included *The Impressionist Landscape from Corot to Van Gogh* and *Andy Warhol: The Celebrity Portraits* featuring three

The *Fountains of Bellagio*, the largest musical water fountain system in the world

decades of celebrity pictures, including Jackie Kennedy, Elizabeth Taylor, Dennis Hopper, Sylvester Stallone and Michael Jackson.

Tel: (702) 693 7871. www.bellagio.com (see p133). Open: Sun–Tue & Thur 10am–6pm, Wed, Fri & Sat 10am–7pm. Tours available Wed–Sun 3.30pm. Admission charge.

Caesars Palace

Caesars Palace is synonymous with Las Vegas. Across the globe, many aspiring nightclubs, penny arcades and casinos have used its famous name in an effort to give their business the excitement and glamour of Las Vegas, but the original Caesars Palace reigns supreme.

Its imperial presence has dominated the landscape since 1966, when the luxury resort based on ancient Rome became the first themed hotel on the Strip. In its 45 years, Caesars Palace has become known for its opulence, with standard guest rooms that include armoires, European-style bathrooms, chaises longues and platform beds, while the suites include dining rooms, in-room saunas and steam rooms.

Since Andy Williams opened the Circus Maximus showroom in Caesars

---

AIR CONDITIONING

All hotels are air conditioned, but can prove quite chilly if you are not used to it. Take an extra layer of clothing if you plan to be sitting in a bar or restaurant for a few hours.

---

in 1966, the Palace has played host to an impressive list of headliners and to many star-studded television shows and specials. Today, the newly completed Colosseum presents shows starring Cher and Jerry Seinfeld.

The main entrance to Caesars Palace is set back a little from the Strip. You can walk through the gardens, ornamented with Roman statues and fountains, or use the moving walkways each side of the property. As in every Las Vegas hotel, from the main entrance you walk right into the casino. One difference with Caesars Palace is that the casino entrance is not surrounded by rows of slot machines, but you will see table games inside. Card dealers and croupiers dress in black and gold, and cocktail waitresses in toga-inspired costumes fuss around the clientele. The slot machines are located to the right of the property in a second casino area.

Between these two casinos there is a selection of restaurants and bars, including the Hyakumi Japanese Restaurant and Sushi Bar, and Cleopatra's Barge, an ornate floating cocktail bar. For fine dining, restaurants include Bradley Ogden, Rao's, Guy Savoy, Sea Harbour, Neros and Mesa Grill. Casual diners can enjoy Serendipity 3, Cypress Market and Augustus Café.

Caesars Palace is also famed for its Forum Shops – over 160 stores and boutiques in a beautiful shopping centre that features Roman architecture and is set beneath an ever-changing deep-blue sky. Children will love the tropical fish tanks and the talking statues, although they are equally captivating for adults if they can resist the lure of stores such as Louis Vuitton, Escada, Gucci, Guess, Christian Dior, Jimmy Choo, Fendi and BOSS HUGO BOSS. A large extension has recently extended the mall to Las Vegas Boulevard.

After dark, Caesars Palace has a vibrant nightlife, with bars and clubs that include PURE, a sophisticated club with renowned DJs; Cleopatra's Barge, an Egyptian-style floating nightclub; liberal servings at the Galleria Bar; erotic silhouette dancers at the Shadow Bar; the Spanish Steps, the outdoor bar and orientation focal point; and the captivating Seahorse Lounge with its seahorse-filled aquarium.

www.caesarspalace.com (see p132).

The vast Caesars Palace complex

Tour: City landscapes

See the world in one city, as the Las Vegas Strip presents famed locations from across the globe. Some hotels have been described as small cities, with accommodation, recreation, nightlife and dining all under one roof, but some resorts have taken the theme literally, presenting their own version of American and European destinations.

Allow one day. Use the Las Vegas monorail to reach some resorts.

1 The Venetian

Your first stop is the beautiful city of Venice, presented in the centre of the Strip with The Venetian Resort & Casino. The architecture is remarkably accurate, presenting Venice landmarks such as the Campanile Tower, St Mark's Square and the Rialto Bridge all connected with replica streetscapes over the Grand Canal, which sweeps through The Venetian in the same way that the water weaves through Venice.

2 Grand Canal Shoppes

You can spend hours wandering through The Venetian streets visiting world-famous retailers. Grab a coffee or a snack in the food hall, or dine in style at Canaletto or Postrio in St Mark's Square. The Venetian is also famed for its street entertainers, who perform throughout the shopping area, and you may even catch a glimpse of the mysterious Sporatto who stalked the real city streets in the 16th century. Your visit would not be complete

without a relaxing ride on the Grand Canal, escorted by a tuneful gondolier.
Open: daily from 10am. Gondola rides daily 10am–11pm, Fri & Sat 10am–midnight.
Head south down the Strip.

3 Paris Las Vegas

Just south of The Venetian you cannot miss the Eiffel Tower standing as an architectural marker for Paris Las Vegas. This resort was once the humble Little

Paris Las Vegas

Caesars, which contained only 150 slot machines compared to over 1,700 clustered around the feet of the Eiffel Tower today. Other Parisian landmarks include the Arc de Triomphe, the Paris Opera House and the Louvre, while the guest towers are inspired by the French capital's Hotel de Ville.

4 *Eiffel Tower Experience*

Make sure you take a trip on the *Eiffel Tower Experience* and see the Strip from 140m (460ft) up. Connecting Paris to

Bally's next door is Le Boulevard, complete with cobblestones and brass lamps, which offers a selection of boutiques in a magnificent Parisian setting. You can stop for coffee in Le Café Île St Louis. Located behind the casino in Paris is Le Village Buffet, acclaimed as one of the best restaurants in Las Vegas (*see p145*).
Open: daily 9.30am–12.30am. Continue south along the Strip until you reach the junction with Tropicana Avenue.

5 New York-New York

Round off the day in New York-New York, the first city-themed resort in Las Vegas and not only acclaimed as the best example of architecture on the Strip but also voted the coolest building in Las Vegas. Stop in at Nine Fine Irishmen and enjoy hearty Irish cuisine, storytelling and real beer, believing you are in Dublin rather than overlooking the Strip. Finally, head back into the Big Apple with the Bar at Times Square and finish off the evening with the duelling pianos and riotous sing-along.
Nine Fine Irishmen opens for dinner from 4pm. Bar at Times Square duelling piano show times Mon–Thur 8pm–3am, Sat & Sun 8pm–4am.

STUDIO 54

Visit New York City's famous Studio 54 in the MGM Grand. Once described as the most famous, outrageous and unique nightclub on earth, Studio 54 has been reborn in Las Vegas (*see p107*).

The Flamingo

Standing proud in the heart of the Las Vegas Strip is the shimmering pink Flamingo Hotel. Its ideal location makes the hotel a favourite for Las Vegas regulars and any visitor who wants to absorb a little Las Vegas history. Originally, all Vegas hotels maintained a Western theme, but in 1946 the arrival of Ben 'Bugsy' Siegel and his fabulous Flamingo Hotel heralded a new age for the city – luxurious casinos, Hollywood glamour and the infiltration of the Mafia.

Along with the Flamingo, crime families from the Syndicate to the Cleveland Mob controlled hotels such as the Sands, the Desert Inn, the Tropicana, the Thunderbird, the Sahara, the Stardust and the Dunes.

Legend places Bugsy Siegel as the founding father of Las Vegas, but the Flamingo was actually the third hotel to appear on the Las Vegas Strip, while the Downtown area of the city was already established as a casino hotspot. In true mob style, Ben Siegel lost his life in pursuit of his desert dream as his bosses took revenge for his lavish expenditure on the property.

Today, with the mob long departed, Harrah's Entertainment owns the Flamingo Hotel. It pays tribute to Ben Siegel with Bugsy's Bar, named in his honour, which is open 24 hours in the casino.

Over the years, the Flamingo has been extensively remodelled and now has more than 3,500 rooms and suites. Nestled within the property is a 6-hectare (15-acre) tropical garden and pool area, which is also home to the Flamingo Wildlife Habitat. More than 300 birds and animals can be found in this tropical setting with waterfalls and lagoons right in the centre of the Strip. Over 30 species of birds live in natural environments, including African penguins, swans, ducks and the hotel's stunning mascot, the Chilean flamingo. There are four swimming pools, including Bugsy's original pool and newer additions with hot tubs, water slides and The Beach Club restaurant.

Fine dining is offered at Steakhouse46 and Hamada of Japan, while casual diners can eat a variety of meals and snacks at the Beach Club, the Sin City Brewing Company, Margaritaville or the bountiful Paradise Garden Buffet.

For entertainment, recent headliners included Donny and

'EVERY MAN HAS HIS PRICE, OR A GUY LIKE ME COULDN'T EXIST'

Howard Hughes is always remembered as eccentric – a famed recluse, ailed with a variety of phobias, medical conditions and a well-documented obsession with cleanliness. In 1966 the Texan-born billionaire arrived in Las Vegas and took up residence on the ninth floor of the Desert Inn, which he quickly purchased along with the Sands, the Castaways, the Landmark, the Frontier and the Silver Slipper. Taking ownership from the Mafia, these historical business transactions finally shifted the ownership of the corrupt desert city from criminal to corporate.

Marie Osmond, along with *The Second City*, improvised comedy at its best from the company that gave us world-class comedians such as John Belushi and John Candy. Innuendo runs riot in *X Burlesque*, a titillating show that incorporates all manner of props, including bungees and beds, into its dance routines.

www.flamingolasvegas.com (see p131).

The famous Flamingo casino

The best views of the Strip

There are several good vantage points to see the best view of Las Vegas Boulevard, or the Strip as it is known today. Day or night, try to catch an aerial view of the city, available from several high-rise locations.

The Stratosphere Tower

At the northern tip of the Las Vegas Strip, the Stratosphere Tower stands at a lofty 345m (1,132ft). The tallest free-standing observation tower in the USA, it is visible from most areas in Las Vegas, and when you see the city skyline from a distance the Stratosphere stands as a marker, with the Strip extending southwards and Downtown Las Vegas clustered beyond it to the north.

At the top of the Stratosphere, the observation deck provides breathtaking views, a lounge to relax in, and fine dining at The Top of the World, a high-rise restaurant that rotates 360 degrees for optimum views of Las Vegas.

The Stratosphere is well known for its thrill rides (*see pp105–6*). If the tower isn't tall enough, the Big Shot fires riders upwards to the very tip of the needle, X Scream propels eight terrified riders headfirst over the tower edge, while Insanity – the Ride spins its passengers face down over Las Vegas.

Open: daily 10am–1am (Fri & Sat until 2am). Admission charge includes unlimited rides.

The *Eiffel Tower Experience*

In the heart of the Strip stands Paris Las Vegas. Beyond its stunning architecture, the interior features cobbled walkways and Parisian streetscapes under a deep-blue sky. Paris was opened in 1999, with 32-storey guest towers that offer magnificent Strip views; if your room is ideally located, you'll be able to see the *Fountains of Bellagio* across the Boulevard.

The hotel is famed for its replicas of the Arc de Triomphe and the Eiffel Tower, which is an exact reproduction of its Parisian counterpart. Visitors can buy admission to the *Eiffel Tower Experience*, which transports you 138m (453ft) upwards to a panoramic view of Las Vegas from the centre of the Strip.

Open: 9.30am–12.30am. Admission charge. Tickets are available at the Eiffel Tower box office on the Strip and in hotel gift shops.

Mon Ami Gabi

Not a high-rise view, but for fine dining alfresco, Mon Ami Gabi offers French cuisine in the warmth of the desert sun. Located at Paris in the middle of the Strip, you can sit outside and watch the world rush by on the Las Vegas Strip, and by night you have the ideal view of the *Fountains of Bellagio.*

Strip tours by helicopter

The greatest aerial view of Las Vegas is from a helicopter. Many tour companies offer helicopter trips to the Grand Canyon or the Hoover Dam, as well as nightly tours of the Las Vegas Strip.
Stars and Stripes Air Tours.
500 East Cheyenne Ave.
Tel: (702) 736 7777/(888) 779 0800.
www.lvhelicopters.com

Night-time helicopter tours provide a stunning view of Las Vegas

The Mirage

The Mirage cost $630 million to build and when it opened in 1989 it was the most expensive casino hotel ever built anywhere in the world. It's since been eclipsed by other even-bigger and costlier hotels, but it still remains one of the great Vegas hotels. Attractions range from its erupting Volcano – as well known in Las Vegas as Bellagio's Fountains – to its hit Cirque du Soleil Beatles' show *LOVE*.

It's not surprising that Mirage had the impact that it did, as it was the first Vegas hotel to be built by Steve Wynn, who has since gone on to become one of the big Vegas names with other hotels such as Wynn

The Mirage Volcano erupts every 15 minutes

Las Vegas and Encore. His Mirage featured gold windows, which were created by incorporating real gold into the manufacturing process that tinted them.

If playing the tables in the casino, make sure you know what you're doing, as some of the games have $500 minimum bets. You can wager on the slots anything from 1 cent to $1,000, and there's a 20-table Poker Room too.

The Mirage Volcano

The nightly eruption of the volcano in front of the Mirage is, like the Bellagio Fountains, one of the must-see free shows in Las Vegas. But even a long-established show like this can't afford to rest on its laurels in Las Vegas, and the volcano was recently given a major make-over. The design team behind the spectacular *Fountains of Bellagio* was brought in to transform the volcano into an even more sensational experience. They recruited the drummer of the legendary Grateful Dead and Grammy Award winner Mickey Hart, to write a soundtrack for the new show in conjunction with the Indian tabla player Zakir Hussain.

In the new show, fireballs are hurled 3.5m (12ft) into the air, and burning lava flows down cracks in the volcano's surface. If you're sitting close to the volcano you can feel an all-too-real heat from the flames, while the new state-of-the-art sound system blasts the music out. If you don't want to be that close to the heat but still want to see the show, book a window table in the restaurant at the Casino Royale, across the street. The show starts daily at 6pm and the volcano erupts every 15 minutes, so you'll get a great view of several performances of the show, all for the price of a dinner.

Siegfried & Roy's Secret Garden

White tigers, elephants and other animals from Siegfried and Roy's collection can be viewed in a natural environment. The Mirage is also home to the **Dolphin Habitat** where Atlantic bottlenose dolphins enjoy an environment that offers a coral reef and 9.5 million litres (2.5 million gallons) of swimming space.
Both open: Mon–Fri 11am–6.30pm, Sat & Sun 10am–6.30pm; summer until 7pm. Admission charge.

www.mirage.com (see p133).

The Venetian

With Italian streetscapes, serenading gondoliers and dining in St Mark's Square or alongside the Grand Canal, Las Vegas has masterfully captured one of the most romantic cities in Europe with the luxurious Venetian. Located on the Las Vegas Strip, close to the junction with Spring Mountain Road and Sands Avenue, The Venetian stands on the former site of the legendary Sands Hotel. With its breathtaking architecture and entertainment, The Venetian is firmly established as one of the great Vegas hotels.

The public areas of The Venetian are split into two main levels. Walk in at street level and you will be astounded by the beautiful ceiling artwork and interior design. The casino and hotel lobby are in this area, as well as bars and restaurants, including Canyon Ranch Café, Canaletto, Delmonico Steakhouse, Tao Asian Bistro and Bouchon. The Grand Lux Café is situated towards the rear of the casino and, with over 150 dishes, it boasts one of the broadest menus in the restaurant industry.

In keeping with all Las Vegas resorts, the hotel offers an impressive selection of fine dining and entertainment, although visitors can also relax in the Canyon Ranch Spa Club. This 6,410sq m (69,000sq ft), two-level health and fitness facility is one of the largest of its kind in North America and is open daily from 6am.

The Venetian features stunning replicas of Venice's architecture

On the second level of The Venetian are the Grand Canal Shoppes, certainly one of the most impressive retail areas in Las Vegas. They can be reached via escalators throughout the casino, or via the Rialto Bridge walkway, located to the right of The Venetian looking from the Strip. With over 46,470sq m (500,000sq ft) of retail space, the shops are set around a reproduction of Venice's Grand Canal, complete with singing gondoliers who serenade visitors under a dusk-blue sky, while the stunning central point of the shopping area is based on St Mark's Square. There are also many coffee shops and restaurants on this level. The recently renovated pool deck boasts 2 hectares (5 acres) of swimming pools and lounging terraces that overlook the Strip.

Madame Tussaud's Las Vegas

For celebrity snapshots, keep your camera handy for Madame Tussaud's Las Vegas, where you can have your photograph taken alongside your favourite stars. There's a whole section of Las Vegas Legends, including the Blue Man Group and Wayne Newton, while Barack Obama has now joined other Presidents including JFK, George W Bush and Benjamin Franklin. The museum is located at the front of The Venetian by the Campanile Tower. *Tel: (702) 862 7800. www.mtvegas.com. Open: daily 10am–10pm. Admission charge.*

www.venetian.com (see p133).

GRAND CANAL SHOPPES ENTERTAINMENT

Street performers, opera singers and costumed entertainers perform throughout the Grand Canal Shoppes and feature:
Artisti del Arté – classically trained performers from across the globe who take you back in time to Renaissance Venice in St Mark's Square from 11.30am.
The Venetian Living Statues – performing daily in St Mark's Square and the Oculus Lounge on the casino level.
Gondoliers – Glide down the Grand Canal in a Venetian gondola from Sun–Thur 10am–11pm, Fri & Sat 10am–midnight.

Wynn Las Vegas

Steve Wynn opened his $2.7 billion resort Wynn Las Vegas in 2005 – compare that with the $630 million his Mirage cost in 1989 when it was the most expensive casino hotel in the world. Not content to rest on his laurels (after all, he had also previously built Bellagio), he added Encore in 2008 at a cost of $2.3 billion.

The two hotels are next to each other. Wynn Las Vegas has about 2,700 rooms and suites, while at Encore the hotelier went for the more exclusive suites-only approach: over 2,000 of them. The largest suites measure up to 540sq m (5,800sq ft), several times the size of a typical American home.

The rooms at Wynn Las Vegas may be smaller but they are still pretty special, with stunning views through complete glass walls. There are 15 restaurants to choose from, including several fine-dining places run by top

(Cont. on p55)

Tour: City of culture

Moulded by the 20th century, Las Vegas has developed its own customs, language, technology, literature and traditions. In a city of make-believe it is hard to imagine that behind the gaming tables, showgirls and all-you-can-eat buffets, Las Vegas is the esteemed home for many priceless works of art.

Allow 5 hours. There are admission charges for these exhibitions.

Start at the Luxor Hotel, 3900 Las Vegas Blvd S.

1 BODIES ... The Exhibition

Showing that Vegas is home to controversial modern art as well as more classic art is this display of human bodies and body parts, presented as artistic pieces. The displays include 13 complete bodies, which have been dissected and preserved, and over 260 organs and other body parts. These include, for example, a healthy lung

displayed next to a black lung that has been badly affected by smoking, and organs that have been damaged by over-eating. While the exhibits are not for the squeamish, it naturally proves popular with children and does show the human body and its parts in a hauntingly beautiful manner.
*Open: daily 10am–10pm
(last admission 9pm).
Head north up the Strip to the Bellagio.*

2 Bellagio Gallery of Fine Art

The elegant Bellagio is a work of art in its own right (*see pp38–40*), but it also houses the Bellagio Gallery of Fine Art, which was opened by developer Steve Wynn in 1998.

The gallery features travelling exhibits from across the globe, and recent exhibitions include *The Impressionist Landscape: From Corot to Van Gogh*, featuring 34 masterworks from the European collection at the Museum of Fine Arts in Boston. A 2010 exhibition is *Figuratively Speaking: A*

Survey of the Human Form, which brings together works from the Bellagio permanent collection, alongside paintings on loan from the Museum of Fine Arts in Boston and the Museum of Contemporary Art in San Diego. Check local guides for the current exhibition. Open: Sun–Thur 10am–6pm, Fri & Sat 10am–9pm. You must be over 18 years old to enter this resort unless you are staying there.
Head north on the Strip to Wynn Las Vegas.

3 The Wynn Collection

Steve Wynn started his impressive art collection in the mid-1990s, which later earned him recognition as one of ARTnews magazine's Top Ten Art Collectors in the world. The original name for his new resort, before he renamed it Wynn, was Le Rêve ('The Dream') after Pablo Picasso's famous painting of his mistress, which is proudly displayed in his collection. Although the price Wynn paid for this 1932 masterpiece is unknown, the previous owner paid $44 million for the painting at Christie's in New York. The priceless Wynn collection of 16th- to 20th-century masterworks includes Vermeer's A Young Woman Seated at the Virginals, one of only 36 Vermeers known to exist, Rembrandt's Self-Portrait, Among the Roses by Pierre-Auguste Renoir, The Persian Robe by Henri Matisse and Steve Wynn (Red, White, Gold) by Andy Warhol. The collection pieces were displayed at the

Wynn Collection Gallery until it was closed in 2006.

The artwork is now on display in various public spaces throughout the Wynn hotel. Steve Wynn made the wrong kind of headlines in 2006 when he accidentally damaged one of his own prize Picasso paintings; he has a degenerative eye condition that makes it difficult for him to see properly. More recently he paid a record price of $35.8 million for a painting by J M W Turner, and a further $33.2 million for a Rembrandt.

A sculpture in the Bellagio gardens

The stunning waterfalls in front of the Wynn Las Vegas

chefs, and even a championship golf course. The resort has two stylish swimming pools joined by a water channel, and a European-style pool where topless sunbathing is allowed – not the norm in a Vegas pool.

Steve and Elaine Wynn's personal and priceless collection of fine art adorns the walls of their luxury resort, which was inspired by Picasso's *Le Rêve* (*see p53*).
www.wynnlasvegas.com (see p134).

Las Vegas Encore

Encore is no less grand. Its casino includes French antiques in its décor, its Italian restaurant Sinatra shows off the original 1953 Oscar that Frank Sinatra won for his acting role in *From Here to Eternity*, and the facilities are topped off with five other restaurants, seven bars and some more of the best swimming pools on the Strip.
www.encorelasvegas.com (see p132).

The north end of the Strip

At the northern tip of the Las Vegas Strip, the Stratosphere Tower stands at a lofty 345m (1,132ft). It is visible from most areas in Las Vegas, and when you see the city skyline from a distance the Stratosphere stands as a marker, with the Strip extending southwards and Downtown Las Vegas clustered beyond it to the north.

At the top of the Stratosphere, the observation deck provides breathtaking views, a lounge to relax in and fine

dining at The Top of the World, a high-rise restaurant that rotates 360 degrees for the optimum views of Las Vegas. The Stratosphere is also home to four of the world's highest thrill rides: the Big Shot, Insanity – The Ride, X Scream and the new and much talked-about SkyJump Las Vegas.

As if the tower wasn't tall enough on its own, the Big Shot fires riders 48m (157ft) upwards to a height of 323m (1,060ft). With a greater G-force than astronauts experience on take-off, the journey takes only 2½ seconds, but your body still wants to fly upwards after the ride has reached its peak. But what goes up must come down, and the ride quickly descends into freefall. Not for the faint-hearted, the Big Shot is the highest thrill ride in the world today. Just the aerial view of Las Vegas will be enough to weaken your knees!

The name Insanity – The Ride speaks for itself. If you're brave enough to attempt it, a 20m (64ft) arm protrudes over the edge of the tower, where it spins passengers facing downwards at an angle of 90 degrees. At the dizzy height of 274m (900ft), and with a force of three Gs, this is the most terrifying way to get an unobstructed view of Las Vegas.

X Scream pushes brave riders to the edge, quite literally. The ride features an open vehicle that propels eight passengers 8.2m (27ft) over the rim of the tower. Riders experience a brief sense of weightlessness as they race towards the ground from a height of

264m (866ft), before the ride drags them back to start all over again.

Finally there's the brand new SkyJump Las Vegas, which lets you do a kind of bungee-jump from the tower using a metal cable, allowing you to fall 260m (855 ft) through the air at speeds of up to 64kph (40mph).

Also at this end of the Strip is the only indoor double-loop, double-corkscrew roller coaster in the USA. The Canyon Blaster reaches speeds of up to 88kph (55mph) inside the Circus Circus Adventuredome.

The Stratosphere is the highest building in Las Vegas

Other attractions
The Auto Collections

More than 250 vehicles are displayed and for sale here in this unique collection, which changes constantly as vehicles are bought and sold. Some of the cars on permanent show include Elvis Presley's 1976 El Dorado, Sammy Davis Jr's Stutz Bearcat, the 1936 Cadillac Limousine that was built new for comedian W C Fields, and a $7 million 1957 Jaguar. The owners are always open to offers on cars so you never know what's going to be there and what isn't – or what new vehicles have been bought in.

Imperial Palace Hotel & Casino, 3535 Las Vegas Blvd S. Tel: (702) 794 3174. www.autocollections.com.
Open: daily 10am–6pm.
Admission charge.

CSI: The Experience

A recent addition to the entertainment options at the MGM Grand is this experience based around the hit US TV series *CSI*. Now it's your chance to become a Crime Scene Investigator, and help solve one of three murders through the clues you'll pick up during the 60–90 minute adventure. You'll also have the use of 15 lab stations and two state-of-the-art forensic crime labs as you try to track down your killers from among the suspects. As well as being a high-tech adventure game, you also get to learn a lot about real crime-scene investigations, including the use of DNA evidence and ballistics.

If you know the show, you'll find some of the characters appearing along the way to move the story on and to help you in your own sleuthing. At the end of the adventure you have to present your findings to the CSI's head investigator, and this is when you discover just how good a TV detective you might make. The experience is recommended for those aged 12 and over, although under-12s are admitted if accompanied by an adult. Numbers are limited, so booking ahead is advisable.

MGM Grand, 3799 Las Vegas Blvd S. Tel: (702) 891 1111. www.mgmgrand.com. Open: daily 9am–10pm, except 1 Jan 10am–5pm (last entry 1 hour before closing). Admission charge.

Las Vegas Natural History Museum
This non-profit organisation presents dinosaur displays, fossils, marine life, Nevada wildlife, world wildlife and an Africa exhibit. Some of the wildlife on display includes tarantulas, scorpions, snakes and lizards. There's also marine life in a 13,600-litre (3,000-gallon) tank, including sharks and sting rays. It's more than just natural history, however, as there is also a section on the Treasures of Egypt, which includes a replica of the entrance to the tomb of King Tutankhamun and of some of the great treasures that were found within. It is one of only two sets of replicas that were permitted by the Egyptian authorities.

900 Las Vegas Blvd N. Tel: (702) 384 3466. www.lvnhm.org. Open: daily 9am–4pm. Admission charge.

MGM Grand Lion Habitat
The MGM Grand would not be complete without the company's trademark, or Leo the Lion as film goers know him, so the hotel presents its own pride of lions. You can watch these magnificent creatures interact with their trainers and study them up close as they laze above a walk-through tunnel. The lions don't actually live full-time in the habitat, but have a much more spacious permanent home on a 3.4-hectare (8.5-acre) ranch outside the city, with different animals being brought in to live in the hotel for a while. The ranch is owned by one of the USA's leading big cat experts and conservationists Keith Evans, who also looks after 26 lions, 3 tigers and 2 snow leopards.

MGM Grand, 3799 Las Vegas Blvd S. Tel: (702) 891 1111. Open: daily 11am–7pm. Free admission.

Titanic: The Artifacts Exhibition
With over 300 artefacts discovered on the *Titanic* and rescued from 4km (2½ miles) below the sea, this huge exhibition includes the personal possessions of its passengers and crew, a 15.25-tonne (15-ton) section of the ship's hull and re-creations of parts of the ship, which include a first-class

(*Cont. on p60*)

Tour: Virtual history

While Las Vegas offers cuisine, culture and entertainment from around the world, you can also travel through the centuries. At Neonopolis you can see into the future with Star Trek: the Experience, *while the Strip transports you back in time to Ancient Egypt, Ancient Rome and medieval England.*

Allow one day. Use the monorails to reach resorts.

1 The Venetian

Beneath reproductions of historic frescoes, Renaissance characters meander through a lavish lobby, dripping with gold and marble. Take a gondola ride along the Grand Canal before enjoying a pasta dish at one of the many Italian restaurants.
Head south along Las Vegas Boulevard for about half a block.

2 Caesars Palace

On the opposite side of the Strip is the magnificent Caesars Palace. Mob aficionados once likened this resort to historic Sicily rather than ancient Rome, but it has undergone many changes in nearly 40 years. In 1967 Evel Knievel attempted to jump the fountains (then the largest in the world) by motorbike, which proved to be a near-fatal stunt. *See also pp40–41.*

3 The Forum Shops

The Roman streetscapes bustle under a changeable blue sky. Several Strip resorts

have adopted this interior concept, but Caesars was the first. 'Shoppus til you Droppus' is their motto, and you can watch statues of Venus, Apollo and Bacchus come to life in an atmospheric display of rain, fire and mist under a

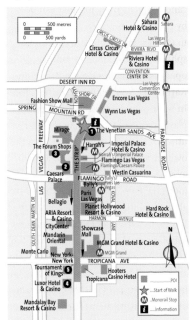

thunderstruck sky. The Forum Shops are also home to a 190,000-litre (50,190-gallon) aquarium and you can take a virtual-reality thrill ride through time with Race for Atlantis.

Open: daily 10am–11pm (weekends until midnight). The Fountain Shows run every hour on the hour.
Retrace your steps along Flamingo Road and turn right down the Strip.
Keep going south until you are past Reno Avenue.

4 Luxor Hotel & Casino

When the Luxor first opened in 1993, its stunning architecture was unlike any other building to appear on the Strip. By night the pyramid emits the world's brightest beam from its tip, a 40 billion candlepower projection that can be seen by pilots in Los Angeles. The entrance to the pyramid is protected by a giant sphinx, while the interior houses an open-plan design reflecting Luxor and Karnak, all finished with hieroglyphics. In recent years, the Luxor has been playing down the Egyptian theme a little, as are some other hotels with their own various themed approaches. But guests still get to their rooms by journeying up 'inclinators', which travel along the interiors of the giant pyramid. Rather less sedate is the IMAX motion simulation ride called 'In Search of the Obelisk', which whizzes passengers into an archaeological dig underneath a pyramid. It turns Howard Carter, who discovered King Tut's tomb, into an Indiana Jones figure. Until recently a replica of King Tut's tomb was on display but now time travellers must make do with the IMAX ride.

5 Tournament of Kings

End your day with an old-fashioned English joust at the Excalibur. Its design is similar to the fairy-tale castle Neuschwanstein, built between 1869 and 1886 for the eccentric King Ludwig II of Bavaria, which also inspired Sleeping Beauty's castle at Disneyland®. Beyond the portcullis and courtyards you can tuck into a messy medieval feast at the Tournament of Kings dinner show, where knives and forks are off the menu and you can shout at a cast of over 100 performers as they lock swords and fight dragons in King Arthur's Arena.

Tel: (702) 597 7600. Shows Mon–Thur 6pm, Fri–Sun 6pm & 8.30pm. Tickets $54.95, includes show and three-course dinner. Book early.

A giant sphinx guards the entrance to the Luxor

The famous Welcome to Las Vegas sign at the southern end of the Strip

cabin and the ship's vast boiler room. Expect there to be additional special exhibitions in the approach to the 100th anniversary of the sinking of the *Titanic*, which occurred in April 1912. *Luxor, 9777 Las Vegas Blvd S. Tel: (702) 796 7111. Open: daily 10am–10pm (last admission 9pm). Admission charge.*

'Welcome to Las Vegas' sign
As famous as the Hollywood sign, the Welcome to Las Vegas sign is the place in Vegas to have your photo taken. It's right at the south end of the Strip, and in fact many people use this as an indication of where the Strip actually stops. Trivia fans like to point out that the Las Vegas sign isn't actually in Las Vegas, but is well outside the city limits in the neighbouring town of Paradise. In fact, a lot of Las Vegas isn't in Las Vegas, if

you want to be picky, as most of the southern Strip is also in Paradise.

Whether it's in Vegas or not, the Welcome sign has been letting people know they've arrived – and providing photo opportunities – since it was put up in 1959. In true Vegas style, it was thought up by a businessman and then sold to the state of Nevada. It's 7.5m (25ft) high, and each letter in the word 'Welcome' is picked out in a circle, meant to be a silver dollar. There's a replica of the sign on the Boulder Highway, and Las Vegas has adapted the sign further along the Strip to provide a different version that welcomes people to Downtown Las Vegas. This, however, is the original, a true icon of the city. There's a small parking area to make access easier, as crossing Las Vegas Boulevard on foot isn't easy, given the heavy traffic.
5200 Las Vegas Blvd S (see map on p63).

Zero G

Several times a year, Vegas gives visitors the chance to try out Zero Gravity, when the Zero G show comes to town. In a specially converted Boeing 747, you get training and 90 minutes of flight time, although not all of this is at Zero G. The plane can also simulate the lower gravities on both Mars (one-third of your weight) and the Moon (one-sixth of your weight), giving you the chance to feel what it's like to walk on the surfaces of both planets. The Zero G flights have, like most things in Vegas, attracted their share of celebrities, including Martha Stewart and Professor Stephen Hawking.

After the pre-flight training on the Strip, guests are taken out to the airport to board the adapted 747. The back of the plane looks fairly normal, but the front half has been converted into an open space where the various degrees of gravity can be created. Specially padded walls ensure soft landings as guests float about the plane, just as if in space, trying to eat sweets and do other tasks that lack of gravity makes difficult. The whole flight is filmed, so you have a permanent record of your time in the air.

Zero G training usually takes place at the Four Seasons Hotel at 3960 Las Vegas Blvd S, with the flights themselves leaving from the Signature Air Terminal at McCarran International Airport. You must be over 15, and in good health. Pregnant women cannot do Zero G flights. For the Flight Schedule listing upcoming Las Vegas dates, see the Zero G website: www.gozerog.com. The cost of training and the Zero G flight is currently around $5,000, plus taxes.

A first-class cabin from the SS *Titanic* as seen at the Luxor

Off the Strip

Away from Las Vegas Boulevard, hotels offer the same glitz and luxury as on the Strip, but the room rates can be extremely competitive. Some of these hotels are only a block or two away and feature attractions that certainly warrant a detour.

West side

Art Encounter

This is Nevada's largest fine-art gallery and has been in business since 1992. It features more than 100 original works from both local and national artists.
5720 South Arville St.
Tel: (702) 227 0220.
www.artencounter.com.
Open: Mon–Fri 8.30am–5pm.
Admission charge.

Erotic Heritage Museum

Not for the prudish, this museum to the west of the Strip has a permanent collection of erotic items and regular exhibitions too. The permanent collection includes film, sculpture, photography, documents, ceramics, murals and old peep arcade machines. Visitors are positively encouraged to write on the walls of the toilets, and contribute any jokes they like.
3275 Industrial Road.
Tel: (702) 369 6442.

www.eroticheritage.org. Open: Wed & Thur 6–10pm, Fri 3pm–midnight, Sat & Sun noon–midnight.
Admission charge.

Palms Casino Resort

On an equally adult theme and almost directly opposite the Rio on West Flamingo Road, Palms is a popular location for stag and hen parties. The nightlife includes the Ghostbar, known for offering the best view of the Strip, the multi-level nightclub and concert venue Rain, and the Glass Bar and Entry Bar at the new Palms Pool complex, where up to 3,000 people can party.
4321 West Flamingo Road.
Tel: (702) 942 7777. www.palms.com

Rio Hotel & Casino

With its vibrant exterior lighting, this Brazilian-themed resort can be seen towering behind the west side of the Strip. The 2,582 guest rooms in this hotel are all suites, with floor-to-ceiling

CAREY AVENUE

LAS VEGAS BOULEVARD NORTH

LAKE MEAD BOULEVARD

RANCHO DRIVE (TONOPAH HIGHWAY)

Las Vegas Wash

LAMB BOULEVARD

VEGAS DRIVE

OWENS AVENUE

South Nevada Zoological-Botanical Park

WASHINGTON AVENUE

ORAN K GRAGSON HIGHWAY

Lied Discovery Children's Museum

Main Street Station

MAIN STREET

Vegas Club Hotel & Casino

BONANZA ROAD

Meadows Mall

Golden Nugget Hotel & Casino and Four Queens

DOWNTOWN

CHARLESTON BOULEVARD

Castaways

FREMONT STREET

Stratosphere Tower

SOUTH EASTERN AVENUE

Dinner in the Sky

SAHARA AVENUE

Boulder Station

VALLEY VIEW BOULEVARD

Circus Circus Hotel & Casino

Sahara

Las Vegas Hilton

INDUSTRIAL ROAD

THE STRIP

Las Vegas Hilton

Las Vegas Convention Center

MARYLAND PARKWAY

DESERT INN ROAD

ARVILLE STREET

SPRING MOUNTAIN ROAD

Erotic Heritage Museum

PARADISE ROAD

INTERSTATE 515

Gold Coast Hotel & Casino

Rio Hotel & Casino

Harrah's/ Imperial Palace

Flamingo/ Caesars Palace

Atomic Testing Museum

FLAMINGO ROAD

DECATUR BOULEVARD

Palms Casino Resort

LAS VEGAS FREEWAY

Bally's/ Paris Las Vegas

M&M's World

HARMON AVE

Hard Rock Hotel & Casino

Donna Beam Fine Art Gallery

WINCHESTER

MOUNTAIN VISTA STREET

The Orleans Hotel & Casino

MGM Grand

GameWorks

TROPICANA AVENUE

SPRING VALLEY

Excalibur Hotel & Casino

Liberace Museum

Luxor Hotel & Casino

PARADISE

RUSSELL ROAD

Mandalay Bay Resort & Casino

RUSSELL ROAD

Art Encounter

'Welcome to Las Vegas' Sign

PATRICK LANE

McCarran International Airport

SUNSET ROAD

SOUTH EASTERN AVENUE

GREEN VALLEY

GREEN VALLEY PARKWAY

LAS VEGAS (BRUCE WOODBURY BELTWAY)

WARM SPRINGS ROAD

LAS VEGAS BOULEVARD SOUTH

Las Vegas Outlet Center

BLUE DIAMOND ROAD

Silverton Casino Lodge Aquarium

| 0 | | 2 kilometres |
| 0 | 1 mile | |

POI

Monorail Stop

Information

Airport

Hospital

N

The flamboyant Rio resort

windows that offer spectacular views of the Strip or the mountains. Guests can also relax at the VooDoo Beach, a multi-level pool complex with waterfalls and bay areas. Renegade magicians Penn and Teller are residents at the Rio, and the resort is also famed for the Show in the Sky, a free attraction that takes place in the hotel's Masquerade Village, with carnival entertainers all performing on themed floats suspended on an overhead track, as stages drop down from above and rise up from the floor level. For a small fee you can even join the cast. The Rio also showcases Bevertainers, singing cocktail waitresses, about 20 per cent of whom are actually men, who perform shows every ten to fifteen minutes.
3700 West Flamingo Road.
Tel: (702) 777 7634.
www.riolasvegas.com

Silverton Casino Lodge Aquarium
The artificial reef and aquarium in the Silverton Casino Lodge features stingrays, sharks and 4,000 tropical fish from across the globe. There are several aquariums and wildlife exhibits throughout this hotel, including the hypnotic jellyfish aquariums in the Mermaid Lounge.
3333 Blue Diamond Rd.
Tel: (702) 263 7777. Interactive feeding shows at 1.30, 4.30 and 7.30pm. The Mermaid Lounge is open weekdays 11am–2am, weekends 24 hrs (under 21s are not permitted in this bar). Free admission.

Southern Nevada Zoological-Botanical Park
This Las Vegas zoo contains 150 plant and animal species, including chimpanzees, wallabies and reptiles. The park also offers Desert Ecotours.
1775 North Rancho Drive.
Tel: (702) 647 4685.
www.lasvegaszoo.com. Open: daily 9am–5pm. Admission charge.

East side
Atomic Testing Museum
Unlikely sounding but fascinating and entertaining museum that recounts the story of the testing of atomic bombs at the Nevada Test Site, which was only 104km (65 miles) from Las Vegas.
755 East Flamingo Rd (just east of Paradise Rd), North Las Vegas.
Tel: (702) 794 5151.
www.atomictestingmuseum.org. Open: Mon–Sat 10am–5pm, Sun noon–5pm. Admission charge.

Dinner in the Sky
You've heard of Sky Diving, but Vegas also now has Sky Dining. Just opened is the Dinner in the Sky experience, where you get a chance to dine up to 55m (180ft) in the air at a table suspended in a special pod, giving amazing views over Vegas as you seem to float above the streets. The table seats 22 people around a central area where your chef, waiter and an entertainer do their work. It gives the phrase 'open kitchen' a whole new meaning. The pod has glass walls,

and the whole experience provides the red carpet treatment. You're collected from and returned to your Vegas hotel, have a pre-dinner reception to meet your fellow diners, and post-dinner access to the Sky Lounge, with souvenir photos thrown in for good measure.

2800 West Sahara Ave. Tel: (702) 257 7303. www.dinnerintheskylv.com

Donna Beam Fine Art Gallery

This gallery is located in the University of Las Vegas and has exhibits of all types of media, from national, international and local artists. It also hosts touring exhibitions.

4505 South Maryland Parkway. Tel: (702) 895 3893. donnabeamgallery.unlv.edu. Open: Mon–Fri 9am–5pm, Sat 10am–2pm. Admission charge.

The Hard Rock Hotel & Casino

Voted one of the coolest places to stay in the world, the Hard Rock Hotel is a rock 'n' roll paradise. Located just east of the Las Vegas Strip, on Paradise Road, the Hard Rock is also home to the celebrated music venue The Joint, which regularly features performances from rock legends such as Aerosmith and Santana. With 657 rooms the Hard Rock may be smaller than some of its Strip competitors, but this venue wins out with style. In keeping with Hard Rock Cafes around the world, this hotel showcases a bountiful display of rock 'n' roll memorabilia from the 1950s until the present day, with artefacts from stars such as Mick Jagger, Jimi Hendrix, Elvis Presley, Madonna and Britney Spears.

4455 Paradise Road. Tel: (702) 693 5000. www.hardrockhotel.com

Las Vegas Hilton

Also on Paradise Road, the Las Vegas Hilton was the largest hotel in the world when it opened as the International Hotel in 1969. It is famed as the Las Vegas home of Elvis Presley, where he played throughout the 1970s. Today, the world's largest Hilton has the Hilton Theater, which hosts stars like Julio Iglesias, Al Green and ZZ Top. Some of the guest rooms have a good view of the Strip, but a northeast view over Sunrise Mountain is certainly worth requesting.

3000 Paradise Road. Tel: (702) 732 5111. www.lvhilton.com

Liberace Museum

One of the most popular museums in Las Vegas, the Liberace Museum displays 18 of his 39 pianos, one of which is made out of toothpicks, along with antiques, costumes and cars belonging to the singer, including a rhinestone-encrusted Rolls-Royce. Some of his extravagant costumes weigh up to 80kg (175lb) and cost in excess of $300,000.

1775 East Tropicana Ave. Tel: (702) 798 5595. www.liberace.org. Open: Mon–Sat 10am–5pm, Sun noon–4pm. Admission charge.

Centre of cool, the Hard Rock Hotel

King of Vegas

Luminous, iconic and sparkling with jewels, Elvis Presley is a true mascot for Las Vegas.

His reign started in the late 1960s. After appearing in a succession of Hollywood films, and eight years after his last concert appearance, Elvis made his live stage comeback at the International Hotel (now the Las Vegas Hilton).

Opening on 31 July 1969, Elvis was booked for a four-week 57-show engagement that broke every box-office record in the city. Following his triumphant opening performance, Elvis's enterprising manager Colonel Tom Parker hastily negotiated a contract with hotel executive Alex Shoofey, which they scribbled across a drink-stained hotel tablecloth and honoured until 1976, when Elvis gave his final performance in the city.

Elvis Presley rocketed to fame in 1956, with his debut single 'Heartbreak Hotel'. As his records

Work or play, Elvis was a frequent visitor to Las Vegas. In 1963 he filmed *Viva Las Vegas* in the city. The film used locations such as the Flamingo and the Sahara, then closed with a wedding scene set in the Little Church of the West, which is now located south of the Las Vegas Strip. Three years later, Elvis returned for the real thing when he broke teenage hearts by marrying Priscilla Beaulieu at the Aladdin Hotel in May 1967.

became million-sellers, and Hollywood beckoned, it seemed fitting that Elvis should appear in Las Vegas, and on 23 April 1956 he made his debut appearance at the New Frontier Hotel.

Compared to his later performances in the 1970s, Elvis's first engagement did little to impress his Las Vegas audience. Previously known as the Last Frontier, the hotel had recently been remodelled into a space-age resort where Elvis appeared in the futuristic new showroom as 'The Atomic Powered Singer'. However, without his usual teenage audience, Elvis did little to distract the gamblers from the lure of the gaming tables.

Thirteen years later, when he stepped back into the spotlight at the International, Elvis finally conquered Las Vegas. He was booked for two

Across the globe, Elvis impersonators far outnumber any other tribute artists. In Las Vegas alone, Elvis can command your wedding services or serve you cocktails, and he even has his own professional skydiving team known as the *Flying Elvises*.

lengthy engagements each year, and he sold out two shows every evening for weeks on end.

No other artist can boast the impact that Elvis had on Las Vegas, and it is still evident today. Whether rocking the lounge bars or headlining the Strip, Elvis is everywhere – proof indeed that, over 30 years after his death, Elvis never truly left the building.

'Elvis' will marry you at the Little White Chapel

Tour: Elvis

You cannot avoid Elvis in Las Vegas. The singer spent many years working in the city, and devoted fans can spend days locating every Elvis sight. Although there have been dramatic changes since Elvis's day, there are still many fascinating landmarks, museums and shows relating to the 'King of Vegas'.

Allow one day. Use the Las Vegas monorail to reach some resorts.

1 The Las Vegas Hilton

Originally known as the International, Elvis made his stage comeback in the hotel showroom on 31 July 1969. As you enter the Hilton, a bronze statue commemorating Elvis's sold-out performances is to your right in front of the casino. The showroom, which was once the largest in the city, still exists and is located behind the casino on the ground floor. Its entrance is in the far right-hand corner, but you will be unable to gain access without a show ticket.

Head south down Paradise Road and turn right on to Convention Center Drive, then left down the Strip, continuing south to The Venetian.

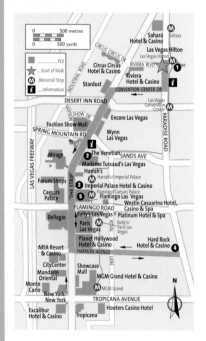

2 Madame Tussaud's Las Vegas (at The Venetian)

Sing with the King and experience Elvis in concert at The Venetian, where you can place a scarf around Elvis's neck or join him on stage for a photo. This waxwork bears an incredible resemblance to Elvis and, if that doesn't make the hairs on your neck stand on end, he'll even talk to you when touched.

Continue south on the Strip.

3 Imperial Palace Hotel

The world's largest classic car showroom at the Imperial Palace Hotel includes Elvis's 1976 El Dorado. Elvis purchased over 100 Cadillacs in his lifetime. The El Dorado coupe was Elvis's vacation vehicle and he added gold wheel covers and engraved the initials TCB (Taking Care of Business) into the doors.

Continue south on the Strip, turn left on Harmon Avenue and walk east.

4 Hard Rock Hotel & Casino

With a huge neon guitar emblazoned across its entrance, this is a must-see resort for any rock 'n' roll fan. The hotel features a unique memorabilia collection, with Elvis items that include film costumes, such as his boxing robe from *Kid Galahad* and his customised 1970 Gibson Dove Guitar. Elvis's caped jumpsuit known as the 'Comet' or 'Adonis' is also part of the collection, he wore it during one of his sold-out shows at Madison Square Garden in 1972. The hotel's collection also includes costumes and artefacts belonging to a wide range of performers, from Bill Haley and Gene Vincent, to Madonna, Kid Rock and the Rolling Stones. Continuing the Elvis theme, it also includes Geri Halliwell's faux Elvis jumpsuit, worn when she appeared with the Spice Girls at the Billboard Music Awards in 1997.

Retrace your steps to the Strip and turn right. Cross over Flamingo Road.

ELVIS IMPERSONATORS

Las Vegas offers a bounty of impersonators and tribute shows to choose from, and you can take your pick from current shows listed in free tourist publications such as *Showbiz*. Perhaps the ultimate tribute was the 2010 opening of the new Cirque du Soleil show, *Viva ELVIS*.

5 Flamingo Las Vegas

Elvis's 15th film, *Viva Las Vegas*, was filmed in 1963 and became his highest grossing movie. Location filming took place in many hotels, including the swimming pool at the Flamingo Hotel.

His influence is everywhere…

Downtown

The city of Las Vegas is barely 100 years old. While the Strip populates the south end of Las Vegas Boulevard, if you follow the road just a couple of kilometres north – past the Stratosphere and a profusion of wedding chapels – a collection of vintage neon signs will welcome you Downtown: to Fremont Street, Main Street and Glitter Gulch. This is where it all started.

It was here in 1905 that the city, fortified by the railroad from Los Angeles to Salt Lake City, was founded. It was later boosted by the construction of the Hoover Dam, the end of prohibition, and legalised gambling.

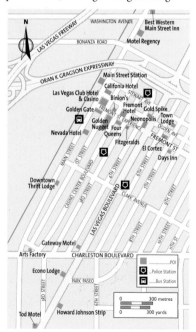

After Downtown started to develop, the first hotels appeared on the Strip, shifting the focus of tourism to the south of the city.

From the northern end of the Strip, how many visitors have looked out from their hotel rooms at that twinkling spot in the distance, and wondered what is out there? The answer is simple – Downtown Las Vegas.

The original Downtown area was once the bustling centre of the city and has now been redeveloped as a celebrated new tourist attraction, with street entertainers, antique neon signs and a unique light show known as the ***Fremont Street Experience***.

This area is also home to many famous Las Vegas establishments, such as the **Golden Gate Hotel**, which opened as the Hotel Nevada in 1906. At the time, rooms in this frontier-style hotel cost $1, and 24 years before gambling was legalised there was not even a casino on the premises. The Golden Gate is also famed for its shrimp cocktails, an appetiser it claims to have introduced to Las Vegas in the 1950s.

Next door on Fremont Street stands the glittering **Golden Nugget**, with its plush white and gold interior. On secure display in the lobby is the Hand of Faith, the world's largest gold nugget. Worth a cool million, this rock was discovered in Australia in 1980. The hotel is also famed for its buffet and is a popular gambling spot for visitors and locals. Just outside its doors,

you have the optimum viewing point for the Fremont Street Experience (*see pp74–6*).

Across the street is **Binion's Gambling Hall**, once known as the legendary Horseshoe. In 1946 the enterprising Benny Binion moved to Las Vegas from Texas, then opened this establishment four years later. Binion pioneered no-limit gambling in the city, along with the 'comps' system, as he worked hard to reward and encourage gamblers, regardless of their budget.

The Plaza Hotel at the tip of Fremont Street

The casino was also famed for launching the World Series of Poker, now held at the Rio, where for an ante of $10,000 players can compete for the ultimate poker accolade and a multi-million dollar prize. Dark and smoky, Binion's does have the ambience of a serious gambling den.

The Arts Factory is a big draw in this arty district where there are numerous galleries, antique shops and exhibition spaces. The monthly First Friday Festival brings up to 15,000 people to the streets here, and there's always something going on. The Arts Factory is home to artists, photographers, sculptors, graphic designers, multi-media artists and others. There's a vintage clothing store here too, and workshops and galleries spread over two floors.
101–109 E Charleston Blvd. Tel: (702) 676 1111. www.theartsfactory.com. Hours vary according to the galleries. Free admission. From the Strip, the Deuce bus route will take you Downtown.

The *Fremont Street Experience*

One of the must-see sights of your visit, the *Fremont Street Experience* started as a $70 million collaboration between the city of Las Vegas and Downtown casinos, and has already evolved considerably.

Before the attraction opened, tourists were always lured to the Strip area and Downtown Las Vegas was almost

> The Fremont Street area is safe for tourists, but be watchful of your belongings when you are distracted by the show. It is advisable not to walk Downtown away from the main streets surrounding the attraction area. If you are driving, valet parking at the **Golden Nugget** is recommended.

forgotten. Now the area has been completely rejuvenated to become an award-winning tourist attraction.

Located between Las Vegas Boulevard and Main Street, this four-block section includes Las Vegas originals such as Binion's Gambling Hall, the California Hotel, Fitzgeralds, the Four Queens, Fremont Hotel, the Las Vegas Club, Main Street Station Casino, the Golden Gate and Golden Nugget. Fremont Street is much smaller than the Strip, with its six lanes of busy traffic, and has been completely pedestrianised, making it easy to visit all the establishments there.

Running four blocks over Fremont Street is the 27m (90ft) high canopy *Viva Vision: The Biggest Big Screen on the Planet.* Previous visitors to Downtown Las Vegas will remember the $70-million *Fremont Street Experience* light show, which was presented on this canopy, until a $17-million expansion in 2004 created the world's largest graphic display system, longer than five football pitches. Set to music, animated displays offer shows that include tributes to music legends such as Don McLean's 'American Pie', the Doors, Queen, Kiss, and a motorcycle ride set to the pounding music of George Thorogood and the Destroyers.

The state-of-the-art LED canopy technology incorporates 12.5 million bulbs, 220 amplifiers capable of producing 550,000 watts of concert-quality sound, 180 high-intensity strobe lights, 64 variable lighting fixtures that can produce more than 300 different colours, 7,000-watt skytrackers, and robotic mirrors that pan and tilt to reflect light.

As each show starts, the businesses on Fremont Street dim their lights and everyone stops still, transfixed by the show above them. Between performances, the area bustles with street entertainers and live music, while you can browse the retail kiosks on the street.

In its formative years Downtown Las Vegas was nicknamed Glitter Gulch, and you will certainly understand this title when you visit. Unlike the computerised façades on the Strip, Fremont Street radiates with neon, and you can feel the warmth of its glow. The whole area is also home to the Neon Sign Museum. Many well-known

Fremont Street on a warm weekend evening

Vegas signs are displayed around here, including the cowgirl Vegas Vicki and her Marlboro-like suitor Vegas Vic (*see below & pp78–9*).

The Fremont Street Experience, 425 Fremont Street. Tel: (702) 678 5777. Viva Vision shows are performed every hour on the hour 6pm–midnight (although this may vary depending on the time of year). There is no admission charge for this attraction and most people stand in the street to watch the show. Restaurant and food prices are very competitive on Fremont Street compared to the Strip.

Neonopolis

For its wealth of luminous signs, the ever-expanding metropolitan area of Las Vegas has often been nicknamed Neonopolis. Along the Strip, computerised billboards compete for your attention, while brilliant high-tech advertisements tower above you, although Downtown Las Vegas seems to have a brighter, warmer glow. It's

The Neon Museum is located on Fremont Street between Main Street and Las Vegas Boulevard. The displays can be viewed for free, but will be far more impressive by night. There are also plaques that explain the history of each sign.

Neonopolis is located at the east end of the *Fremont Street Experience*, where Fremont Street meets Las Vegas Boulevard. *450 Fremont Street. Tel: (702) 477 0470. Open: Sun–Thur 11am–9.30pm (food court closes 7pm), Fri–Sat 11am–10pm (food court closes 10pm).*

in this area, on Fremont Street, between Main and Las Vegas Boulevard, that you can view the original Las Vegas greetings and the most recognisable symbol for the desert city: Vegas Vic.

Vegas Vic was created by the Young Electric Sign Company (YESCO) and erected on top of the Pioneer Club in 1951. This mechanical cowboy was a trusted promotional tool for Las Vegas as his 'Howdy Pardner' greeting had been used on matchboxes, postcards and advertisements since World War II. In its time, Vegas Vic was the largest mechanical sign in the world, as its arm waved a welcome to visiting tourists. If you tried to get a good night's sleep in the area, it was likely to be disturbed by Vic's oft-repeated catchphrase.

Thomas Young Senior created YESCO in 1920, then in 1931 when gambling was legalised he travelled through the Las Vegas area and saw an open marketplace, which his company would later dominate. Designing most of the famed signs in the city, Thomas Young worked from his own sketches and many of his creations still line the streets Downtown, where they are featured in a 4.8km (3-mile) Neon Museum that showcases vintage signs from the heyday of Las Vegas. The Hacienda horse and rider, which once glistened upon the site where Mandalay Bay now stands, has been restored Downtown, along with the sparkling magic lamp from the original Aladdin Hotel, now the Planet

Hollywood Las Vegas, in a radiant presentation of vintage neon signs. Many more classics are still in the restoration process.

Today, Las Vegas is dominated by computerised signs, with Fremont Street's Viva Vision towering over Vegas Vic and Thomas Young's other original creations.

The name Neonopolis has now been adopted by a 23,000sq m (250,000sq ft) entertainment complex, modelled after San Diego's Horton Plaza. Three storeys high and emblazoned with neon, the building is home to Las Vegas Rocks, a combination of restaurant and live music venue, and the Telemundo TV studio. **Star Trek: the Experience** has recently opened here, but there are currently still several other empty venues that are awaiting tenants.

Neonopolis entertainment complex

Tour: Glitter Gulch

The best time to see Downtown Las Vegas in all its glory is by night. Known as Glitter Gulch, the best and most sparkling attractions are all free and all contained within an area that can easily be walked in a short space of time.

Allow one evening. Start from the junction of Las Vegas Boulevard and Fremont Street. You can reach Downtown from the Strip using the Deuce bus service.

1 Neon Museum

Carefully restored, the Neon Museum starts at the end of the *Fremont Street Experience* canopy where the road meets Las Vegas Boulevard. From here, take a walking tour of the signs along the length of Fremont Street. The **Hacienda Horse and Rider**, the first display on this intersection, once stood outside the Hacienda on the Strip, where it was installed in 1967. **Aladdin's Lamp** first appeared on the original Aladdin Hotel when it opened in 1966. The **Flame Restaurant** sign

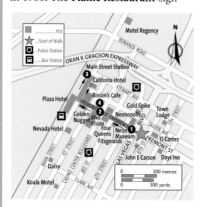

was installed on the Desert Inn Road in 1961. The **Chief Hotel Court** sign on the northwest corner of 4th Street was originally installed on East Fremont Street in 1940. Opposite, **Andy Anderson**, the playful mascot for the Anderson Dairy, was installed in 1956 on their premises on Las Vegas Boulevard. Dating from the 1940s, the original location for the **Wedding Information** sign is unknown. **Red Barn** dates from around 1960, but although the sign was saved the Red Barn bar on Tropicana Avenue burnt down. Dating from around 1950, the **Nevada Motel** sign features the first appearance of Vegas Vic. **Dot's Flowers** was originally located on Las Vegas Boulevard in the 1940s, while the 1946 **5th Street Liquor** sign hails from a Downtown establishment on Las Vegas Boulevard.

Open: 24 hours. New additions are always made to this museum, which offers more exhibits in Neonopolis. Continue west along Fremont Street.

Neon cowgirl in Glitter Gulch

2 *Viva Vision*

Browse Fremont Street establishments such as the Four Queens, Fitzgeralds or the Golden Nugget under their LED canopy (*see pp74–6*) until the light show starts every hour on the dot. There are also traders and entertainers in the street, and you can enjoy live music (local magazines will list the current entertainment schedule). Most people stand to watch the show, but for a more comfortable view, grab a coffee and sit outside Starbucks at the Golden Nugget.

Go to the end of Fremont Street and turn right on to Main Street. Main Street Station is at 200 North Main Street.

3 Main Street Station

Make sure you find the time to see the unusual antiques and memorabilia in this casino, which include curiosities such as Theodore Roosevelt's railroad car and a section of the Berlin Wall. Stop off at the Triple 7 Restaurant and Brewery and sample their speciality beers, oysters or garlic-and-herb French fries.

Retrace your steps back along Main Street, and turn left on to Fremont Street until you reach Binion's Gambling Hall at 128 Fremont Street.

4 Binion's Café

For a late stop and some of the best steaks in town, call in at Binion's Café. The Café is in the basement of Binion's Gambling Hall but if you want views then go to the Binion's Ranch Steakhouse on the 24th floor, where you can gaze out across the Las Vegas Valley.

Binion's Café is open daily 24 hours. The Binion's Ranch Steakhouse opens daily 5.30–10.30pm.

Historic Las Vegas

North of Fremont Street, just a few blocks from Vegas Vic, the Golden Nugget and a multi-million-dollar light show, stands an old Mormon fort. It is protected within a State Historic Park, quite tiny in comparison to other national treasures, but represents the place where Las Vegas began.

For thousands of years, a small oasis in the middle of the desert supplied water for travellers, and was a meeting point for the native Paiute. The underground source was 6km (4 miles) away, but the water bubbled to the surface and formed a small creek and river that disappeared into the desert. The area

Where it all began

was named Las Vegas, or 'the meadows', and in 1855 a team of Mormon missionaries built the first permanent structure on the desert landscape. A fort was built from sun-dried bricks under the leadership of William Bringhurst, and served as a post office and resting point for travellers, heavily guarded with 45m (150ft) walls and two lookout towers. With the creek's resources, the Mormons grew crops and tended an orchard, but abandoned the fort due to harsh desert temperatures and discord within the group.

In 1865 Octavius D Gass occupied the land. Using materials from the abandoned fort he built a ranch house, and ran a blacksmith's forge and a shop that sold beef, vegetables and fruit. He financed his land purchases with a loan from Archibald Stewart at an extortionate 30 per cent interest rate that Gass was unable to meet – so in 1881 the ranch became the possession of his creditor. Three years later, Archibald's wife Helen Stewart inherited the 720 hectares (1,800 acres) after her lover murdered her husband during a so-called act of self-defence.

As a main rail line was planned for the state, Helen Stewart predicted a boom in the desert area. She hired civil engineer James McWilliams, who made large land purchases and sold lots to the west of the proposed rail line, creating the original Las Vegas town site in 1904. Reaching Las Vegas in 1905, the rail line was owned by Senator William Clark, who created a new town plan on the east side of the line instead. Over 3,000 prospective buyers attended Clark's public auction, while many of the original residents simply picked up their wooden properties and dragged them across the rail tracks to the new

Las Vegas on the east. With credit to Clark, the thriving new city of Las Vegas was officially founded in 1905.

Today, the Old Las Vegas Mormon Fort is open to the public. The ranch house no longer exists, but part of the fort still remains and there are replicas of pioneer gardens, a corral and a museum detailing the history of the site. In 1929 part of the fort was used as a concrete testing lab for the construction of the Hoover Dam. *Old Las Vegas Mormon Fort, 500 East Washington Ave. Tel: (702) 486 3511. The park is open Tue–Sat 8.30am–4.30pm. Admission is inexpensive and there are guided tours at 11am & 1pm. There is no charge for children under 12.*

The corral at the Old Las Vegas Mormon Fort

Tour: Las Vegas origins

Although the city is still rapidly developing, there are many historic places of interest left in Las Vegas.

Allow one day.

Many of these sights are located around the Downtown area of Las Vegas. Sights 2–5 can be reached on foot from Fremont Street, but to see the rest of the sights you will need your own car or other transport. You can reach Downtown from the Strip using the Deuce bus service.

Start at the Old Las Vegas Mormon Fort on Washington Ave. CAT bus route 113 runs up Las Vegas Boulevard to Washington Ave from the Downtown Transportation Center in Stewart Ave.

1 Old Las Vegas Mormon Fort

Start your tour in the area of the Las Vegas Creek, where the Mormon missionaries built their adobe fort in 1855. Parts of the original fort still remain and there is a museum with

information on the succeeding occupants and the founding of Las Vegas (*see pp80–81*).
500 East Washington Ave. Go down Las Vegas Boulevard, and turn right on Fremont Street.

2 Golden Gate Hotel & Casino

First opened in 1906 as Hotel Nevada, later to be renamed Sal Sagev. If you are puzzled by this name, read it backwards.
1 Fremont Street.
Go back along Fremont Street.

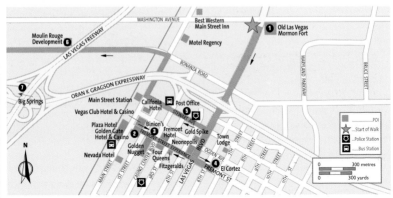

CLARK COUNTY MUSEUM

Outside Las Vegas, in Henderson, the **Clark County Museum** details the area's history, including Boulder City, Las Vegas and the formation of Henderson as a location for bomb production in World War II. The museum includes restored buildings among its fascinating artefacts.

Clark County Museum, 1830 South Boulder Highway, Henderson. Tel: (702) 455 7955.

3 Binion's Gambling Hall

Binion's, 'the place that made poker famous', has been on Fremont Street since 1951.

128 Fremont Street.
Continue in the same direction along Fremont Street until just past 6th Street.

4 El Cortez Hotel & Casino

Built in 1941 at a cost of $245,000, this was the first major resort in Las Vegas and today its exterior remains unaltered.

600 Fremont Street.
Head back west along Fremont Street and turn right on to Las Vegas Blvd. Continue along until you reach East Stewart Ave, then turn left.

5 Post Office/Federal Building

This impressive building just behind Fremont Street was built in 1933. It is now home to a new cultural centre, including a mob exhibition championed by Mayor Oscar Goodman.

301 East Stewart Ave.
CAT bus route 106 runs past the
Moulin Rouge from the Downtown Transportation Center on Stewart Ave.

6 The Moulin Rouge Hotel & Casino

Listed on the National Register of Historic Places, the Moulin Rouge opened in 1955 and was the first desegregated casino in Las Vegas. A fire destroyed the building in 2003, but redevelopment plans are under way in 2010.

900 West Bonanza Rd.
CAT bus routes 402, 207 and 104 (towards Meadows Mall/Valley View) run to Big Springs, approx. 5km (3 miles) west of the Moulin Rouge.

7 Big Springs

Where John Fremont recorded the discovery of Las Vegas. These springs provided all the water for Las Vegas until Lake Mead was used as a resource.

Valley View Blvd, between Alta Drive and US 95.

El Cortez was the first Las Vegas resort

Tour: Las Vegas origins

What Makes Vegas Vegas

Nowhere else on earth has everything that Vegas can offer. There may be better theme parks in Florida or southern California, and there are casinos all over the USA; there are nightclubs in every city in the world, and there are certainly more romantic wedding venues. But nowhere else pulls all these things together, and then throws in more superstars than Hollywood, adds celebrity chefs galore, and produces such daring architecture under so much neon glare. It's what makes Vegas Vegas – and unique.

All that glitters

Las Vegas has welcomed some of the world's greatest superstars to its showrooms, and many have proved to be as glittering and ostentatious as the illustrious hotels that headlined them. A visit to Las Vegas would not be complete without honouring some of the stars that have played the city, and there are many tribute shows, including *Legends in Concert* at Harrah's, a popular tribute to stars ranging from Dolly Parton to Elvis and Madonna. However, for a real glimpse of Las Vegas glamour, there are two stars that cannot be overlooked.

Wayne Newton

Wayne Newton has been performing in Vegas since 1959, when he skipped school for a two-week engagement at the Fremont Hotel with his brother Jerry. Two weeks soon turned into six years and started a series of some 30,000 solo engagements that culminated in a ten-year contract with the Stardust hotel, which was amicably terminated in 2005 when the hotel was demolished. Along with his brother, Wayne had his own TV show at the tender age of 15, and in 1967 Howard Hughes signed him to a contract that saw him perform up to three shows a night at the Sands, Desert Inn and the Frontier, all adding weight to his well-deserved title of Mr Las Vegas.

ENTERTAINMENT

Legends in Concert
Harrah's Las Vegas, 3475 Las Vegas Blvd S. Tel: (702) 369 5111 for reservations. Shows: Sun, Tue & Thur 6.30pm, 7.30pm & 10pm.

Wayne Newton
Wayne recently auditioned Las Vegas hopefuls in the US television reality show *The Entertainer*. Las Vegas is home to his Casa de Shenandoah Ranch and he performs regularly in the city when he is not on tour.

The Liberace Museum
1775 East Tropicana Ave. Tel: (702) 798 5595. Open: Tue–Sat 10am–5pm, Sun noon–4pm. Admission charge.

Liberace

A child prodigy and master of the honky-tonk piano, Liberace first came to Las Vegas in the 1940s, when he was offered a job at the Last Frontier for $750 a week. As his fame grew, Liberace was commanding over $400,000 a week to appear in his bombastic rhinestone costumes, with his trademark candelabra on top of the piano. Also a master chef, Liberace lived, partied and entertained in Las Vegas until 1986, when he gave his last performance at Caesars Palace.

Today, you can see some of his sparkle at The Liberace Museum, just off the Strip on East Tropicana Avenue (*see p66*).

The museum has recently been refurbished and operates as a non-profit organisation to support the Liberace Foundation for the Performing and Creative Arts.

What Makes Vegas Vegas

The Liberace Museum

Las Vegas in the movies

Hollywood moguls have always been attracted to Las Vegas. As well as investing in property, Tinsel Town big shots have used the city as a luminous backdrop for many classic films, including Jane Russell and Victor Mature in *The Las Vegas Story*, Elvis Presley in *Viva Las Vegas* and Johnny Depp in the dark tale *Fear and Loathing in Las Vegas*.

'In any other town, they'd be the bad guys'

The classic casino heist *Ocean's Eleven* has been filmed twice in Las Vegas. The original movie was made in 1960, starring Frank Sinatra as World War II veteran Danny Ocean, who teams up with his ex-army buddies to rob the five major casinos in Las Vegas, then the Sands,

The Circus Circus hotel was a location for *Diamonds Are Forever*

Desert Inn, Flamingo, Sahara and Riviera. In 2001 the film was remade with George Clooney in the starring role, and on this occasion the gang robbed the Bellagio, the Mirage and the MGM Grand. The remake also starred Brad Pitt, Elliott Gould, Matt Damon and Julia Roberts. Although the sequel, *Ocean's Twelve*, was mostly set in Europe, the boys were back in Vegas for *Ocean's Thirteen*. To watch the films provides a glimpse of how the city has evolved over 40 years.

Diamonds Are Forever

Investigating a worldwide smuggling operation, James Bond visits Las Vegas to uncover casino owner Ernst Stavro Blofeld. Released in 1971 with Sean Connery as 007, *Diamonds Are Forever* was filmed on location at Circus Circus, the Las Vegas Hilton and the Tropicana.

Honeymoon in Vegas

This movie stars Nicholas Cage, James Caan and Sarah Jessica Parker. Cage plays the hapless Jack Singer, who is unable to repay a huge debt after losing a poker game to Tommy Corman (James Caan). Although Jack is in Las Vegas to marry his girlfriend, the only way that he can settle his loss is to allow Corman to spend the weekend with his fiancée Betsy. This hilarious caper was filmed on

LAS VEGAS ON TV

Las Vegas makes frequent television appearances and has been seen in *The X Files*, *The A Team*, *The Partridge Family*, *The Ed Sullivan Show* and *Perry Mason*. Recent appearances include the hit series *CSI: Crime Scene Investigation* and *Las Vegas* starring James Caan.

the Strip in Bally's and also features 34 flying Elvises.

Casino

'No one stays at the top forever' was the tagline of this 1995 film, which dramatised real-life events that took place at the Stardust Hotel, with the mob's inside man Frank 'Lefty' Rosenthal, his wife Geri, and the hot-tempered enforcer Tony 'The Ant' Spilotro. These three roles were played by Robert De Niro, Sharon Stone and Joe Pesci, and the film was directed by Martin Scorsese on location at the Jockey Club, the Riviera and the since-demolished Landmark.

Vegas Vacation

Chevy Chase stars as the half-witted Clark Wilhelm Griswold Jr, whose family heads off to Las Vegas. Their clownish adventures take them to the MGM Grand, the Riviera and the Mirage, where Clark has a close encounter with Siegfried & Roy's white tigers and his wife is charmed by Wayne Newton.

Girls! Girls! Girls!

Las Vegas has always been known for its beautiful showgirls, and has become the celebrated home to several erotic revues. Theatre audiences first saw topless showgirls in 1957 when Minsky's Follies opened their *Holiday for G Strings* production at the Dunes – a cause of great controversy, but a huge commercial success that ran for more than four years and kick-started the demand for adult entertainment in Las Vegas.

The longest-running show on the Las Vegas Strip was Tropicana's *Folies Bergère*. Appearing in the hotel's Tiffany Theater twice nightly, the show presented first-rate variety acts featuring the city's top showgirls, although the earlier performances had fully clothed dancers. After almost 50 years of shows, the Folies finally closed in March 2009.

Another long-established Las Vegas production is *Bottoms Up* at Fitzgerald's, the only topless afternoon show. This highly acclaimed production has been voted best afternoon show and applauded for its value for money, with tickets priced at almost a quarter of other leading revues. Entertainer Breck Wall founded this musical comedy in Dallas in 1959 before moving the show to Las Vegas five years later. With its Vaudevillian theme, delivering old-fashioned laughs, the cast includes several comic regulars with male and female dancers.

BOYS! BOYS! BOYS!

And for the ladies, Las Vegas delivers the *Chippendales* at the Rio, *American Storm* at the V Theater and Australia's *Thunder Down Under* at the Excalibur.

Direct from the Crazy Horse in Paris, where it has been an attraction since 1951, *Crazy Horse Paris* is described as an adults-only exploration of sensuality. Appearing at the La Femme Theater at the MGM Grand, 12 ballet-trained members from the original Crazy Horse production open the show decked out in British military uniform and singing 'God save our bare skins' to the tune of the British national anthem, before the show goes on to use film projections and lighting effects to bathe the dancers' bodies in a multitude of colours and patterns. Audience members must be over 18 to see this show, where the dress code is described as business-casual.

On the same theme, other Las Vegas revues include *Fantasy* at the Luxor and topless vampires in *Bite* at the Stratosphere.

Finally, in true Sin City style, Tropicana Avenue is now the site of Las Vegas's Hooters Casino Hotel. Famed for its singing, hula-hooping, all-American Hooters girls, the company has inspired more than 435 beach-themed restaurants in 45 states (now owned by two different companies), and even has its own airline.

A showgirl mural outside Harrah's casino

Tour: After dark

Known as a 24-hour city, Las Vegas really comes to life after dark. Wander through a casino at any hour, even 4am, and you will see riotous dice games and weary gamblers still trying to even up their percentages on the blackjack tables. Some of the Strip's greatest attractions are offered during the twilight hours and the city is famed for its huge variety of night-time entertainment.

Allow one evening.

1 Monte Carlo

Start your evening in the French Riviera at the Monte Carlo Resort. Inspired by the Place du Casino in Monte Carlo, the whole resort is one-tenth of the size of Monaco and offers European roulette tables, which have only one zero on the wheel compared to American wheels with the zero and double-zero options. Any adept gambler will explain that this slightly increases the player's percentage against the casino. The Monte Carlo is home to acclaimed gourmet restaurants such as

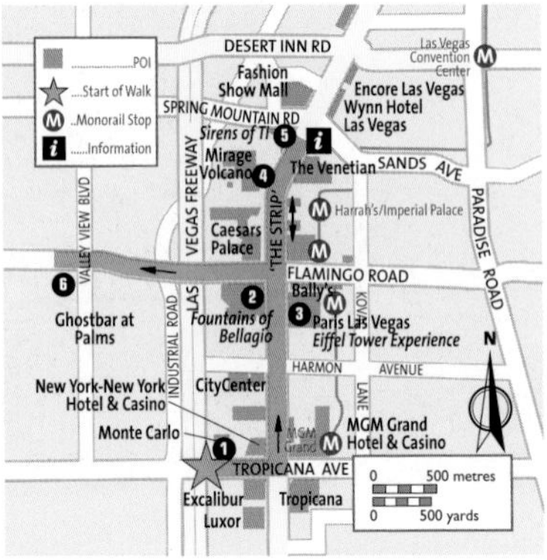

Andre's, with its mouthwatering French cuisine and décor, along with the BRAND Steakhouse and Loungs. Watch chefs prepare your chosen dishes at The Buffet at Monte Carlo, acclaimed as one of the best on the Strip, or brave a close encounter with an 8.2m (27ft) Sin City she-devil in Monte Carlo's latest hotspot, Diablo's Cantina, which serves southern-style American specialities.
Go east on Tropicana Ave, then turn left on to the Strip and head north until just before the junction with Flamingo Road.

2 *Fountains of Bellagio*

This wonderful display starts at 3pm (Sat–Sun at noon), but is far more impressive by night (*see p38*).
Go across the street.

3 *Eiffel Tower Experience*

Even if you have seen this attraction by day, by night Las Vegas is a whole new city. Travel 100 storeys above the city to the top of this Parisian landmark and see Las Vegas in all its neon glory.

Map legend and labels:

POI
★ ...Start of Walk
Ⓜ ...Monorail Stop
ℹ ...Information

DESERT INN RD
Las Vegas Convention Center Ⓜ
Fashion Show Mall
SPRING MOUNTAIN RD
Encore Las Vegas
Wynn Hotel Las Vegas
Sirens of TI ❺ ℹ
Mirage
Volcano ❹
The Venetian SANDS AVE
VEGAS FREEWAY
THE STRIP
Ⓜ Harrah's/Imperial Palace
Caesars Palace
Ⓜ
VALLEY VIEW BLVD
FLAMINGO ROAD
Bally's Ⓜ
❻
Ghostbar at Palms
Fountains of Bellagio ❷
Paris Las Vegas
Eiffel Tower Experience
PARADISE ROAD
KOVAL LANE
HARMON AVENUE
New York-New York Hotel & Casino
INDUSTRIAL ROAD
CityCenter
Monte Carlo ❶
Ⓜ MGM Grand
MGM Grand Hotel & Casino
N
TROPICANA AVE
Excalibur Tropicana
Luxor
0 ___ 500 metres
0 ___ 500 yards

Open: daily 9.30am–12.30am.
Head north on the Strip, past the
Forum Shops.

4 Mirage Volcano

Every evening the peaceful waterfalls outside this Polynesian-themed resort transform into a volcanic eruption with fiery red lights, gas jets and explosions that reach 30m (100ft). This is a very popular attraction, so find your place early, preferably at the end of the previous eruption.
Free shows every 15 minutes,
8pm–midnight (from 6pm in winter).
Continue north on the Strip.

5 *Sirens of TI*

What used to be a rollicking family adventure show along the lines of *Pirates of the Caribbean* is now a more adult-style show. The fantastic special effects are still there, but now the Sirens are far more seductive and wearing far fewer clothes, and the pirate ship features a huge and completely nude figure-head. *Sirens of TI* is now emphatically an after-dark experience.
Show times: 5.30pm (winter only),
7.00pm, 8.30pm, 10.00pm & 11.30pm
(summer only) in Sirens' Cove at the
front entrance of TI – Treasure Island
Hotel and Casino.
Grab a taxi and head to the Palms resort
on West Flamingo Road.

6 Ghostbar at Palms

The Ghostbar on the 55th floor has 3.6m (12ft) floor-to-ceiling windows and the sky deck offers a 360-degree view of the Strip. This is a popular bar, so get there early if you don't want to queue.
Open: daily 8pm–early morning.

Tour: After dark

The Monte Carlo Resort transports you to Monaco

Las Vegas magic

Magic shows are big business in Las Vegas. Signs advertising hotel attractions flicker with images of illusionists and big-budget stunts from some of the greatest names in sorcery.

One legendary Las Vegas duo, who are recognised globally as a symbol for the city, are **Siegfried & Roy**. Featuring 'royal' white tigers and other rare breeds of wild cats, Siegfried & Roy's celebrated stage show ran at the Mirage for 13 years with 5,750 sold-out performances, earning them the title of Magicians of the Century. The show reached a sudden end in October 2003, when illusionist Roy Horn was attacked on stage by his white tiger Montecore. Although the show has ended, they continue to preserve the rare cats in their care, and have dedicated a 32-hectare (80-acre) estate to their animals, along with **Siegfried & Roy's Secret Garden** at the Mirage (*see p49*).

Renegade magicians **Penn & Teller** are in residence at the Rio. Working together for over 30 years, they describe themselves as 'a couple of eccentric guys who have learned to do a few cool things'.

They are award-winning stars of television and Broadway, best-selling authors and several times winners of the Las Vegas Magicians of the Year. Their show features escape acts, stunts with knives, showgirls and even a gorilla, before the two friends shoot each other with .357 Magnums and catch the bullets in their teeth.

Then, if you are ever curious to see how a live goldfish can appear over an audience member's head, visit **Mac King's** act at Harrah's, including visual comedy, sleight of hand and great entertainment for one of the most competitive prices on the Strip.

The hottest magician on the Strip is **Lance Burton**, who resides at the Monte Carlo, in the plush $27-million Lance Burton Theatre. An expert in his craft, his breathtaking family show often enlists the help of audience members, as he makes objects appear, disappear or levitate before their eyes and even makes a car vanish into space.

When he's not walking through the Great Wall of China or making the Statue of Liberty disappear, **David Copperfield** appears as a headliner in Las Vegas. Acclaimed as the greatest

TOP SHOWS

Penn & Teller appear daily (except Tuesday). Tickets are moderately priced, although the show is not suitable for children.
Rio All-Suite Hotel & Casino, 3700 W. Flamingo Rd. Tel: (702) 777 7776.
Lance Burton performs Tues–Sat 7pm. Tickets are moderately priced for this high-quality family entertainment.
Lance Burton Theatre, Monte Carlo Resort & Casino, 3770 Las Vegas Blvd. South. Tel: (702) 730 7160.
Xtreme Magic starring Dick Arthur can be seen Sun–Thurs 2pm & 4pm (late shows on Fri) at the Tropicana Hotel. *3801 Las Vegas Blvd. Tel: (800) 829 9034.*
See your hotel box office or local magazine listings for all current shows.

illusionist of his time, his recent engagements have included the MGM Grand. Copperfield is also based in Las Vegas, where he owns the International Museum and Library of the Conjuring Arts (not open to the public).

US comedian and magician Mac King performs his unique act at Harrah's

Tour: Las Vegas fantasy

In 1989 visionary Steve Wynn started a new era of resort building when the Mirage opened on the Strip. A wave of themed successors quickly followed in the shape of the Excalibur, Luxor, MGM Grand and Treasure Island. It changed the course of history for Las Vegas, offering resorts that didn't just cater for gamblers but created a fantasy world for all the family.

Allow half a day.

1 MGM Grand

With 5,000 rooms, this creation of MGM magnate Kirk Kerkorian was the largest hotel in the world when it opened, costing a million dollars for

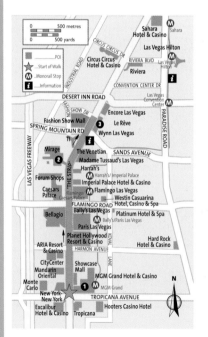

each day of construction. Still one of the largest hotels in the world, this Hollywood-themed resort is spacious and easy to negotiate for visitors, with pictures of Hollywood starlets and leading men gracing the walls. The ceiling above the main casino is decorated with a Tinsel Town mural, and even the MGM trademark lion is honoured with the MGM Grand Lion Habitat (*see p57*).

Head north along the Strip to the Mirage.

2 Mirage

At a cost of $630 million, Steve Wynn opened the Mirage in 1989, a resort he stated would bring people to Las Vegas in the same way that Disneyland® attracted visitors to Orlando. Fronted by a 1.2-hectare (3-acre) lagoon and volcano, the resort's palm-tree-lined drive leads visitors into a South Seas paradise. There's a tropical atrium over 27m (90ft) high, with waterfalls, exotic

HOW MANY BEDS?

It would take nearly 14 years to spend a night in each bed at the MGM Grand, and if you stacked each bed in a pile you could create a tower over ten times as high as the Empire State Building.

palms, orchids and flora, alongside bubbling lagoons and a 91-litre (20,000-gallon) aquarium containing over 90 species of tropical fish. The Mirage is also home to Siegfried & Roy's Secret Garden and Dolphin Habitat, as well as their beloved White Tiger Habitat.

Stop for an epic meal at the Samba Brazilian Steakhouse, where dinner is served daily from 5–10.30pm. Or for more Zen sophistication, try Japonais for innovative sushi in a stylish setting. *Continue north along the Strip till you reach Wynn Las Vegas.*

3 *Le Rêve: A Small Collection of Imperfect Dreams*

Book tickets for this incredible show created by Steve Wynn and the award-winning Franco Dragone. Described as visually stunning and featuring artists and athletes from around the globe, the theatre's unique round design allows every audience member to be centre stage.
Wynn Las Vegas, 3131 Las Vegas Blvd S. Tel: (702) 770 7000. Shows Fri–Tue 7pm and 9.30pm.

Tour: Las Vegas fantasy

A rare white tiger at Siegfried & Roy's White Tiger Habitat

Gambling in Las Vegas

Almost 90 per cent of Las Vegas visitors will gamble. They will spend around $500 each trip and take refuge for four to five hours a day in the casino. Of course, there are those who visit Las Vegas with the sole purpose of gambling, placing thousands of dollars in the casinos' hands as they win, but ultimately lose, for days on end. Then there is the professional gambler, planning to win big in poker or conquer the casinos with blackjack strategy.

Customers are rewarded in Las Vegas. Whether you are on a slot machine or in a high-stakes card game, drinks will be served for free for as long as you keep playing. You will have to tip your cocktail waitress, but the casino will treat you favourably in order to keep your business. Establishments may offer free food, show tickets or accommodation if they see you as a preferential customer. Known as 'comps', these benefits are calculated using your average bet, the time you spend gambling, and the expected house profits from your play. Big-money gamblers, or high rollers, are the most coveted by casinos, who will pick up the cost of luxury suites, limousines, fine dining and entertainment.

Before you play

Any player can benefit from comps if they sign up for a free players' club membership. You will be given a card,

Balloon advertising Paris attractions

Slot machines and tables at the Main Street Station Casino

similar in design to a credit card, which can be placed in slot or video machines as you play, and which can also be used in table games to earn points that can be redeemed for a variety of benefits. As large corporations operate many of the Las Vegas casinos, points can be earned or redeemed throughout the group.

THE GOLDEN RULES OF GAMBLING

- do not gamble beyond your means
- never try to win back your losses
- set a budget for gambling and stick to it.

Most casinos will offer gaming lessons for free, particularly for complicated table games such as craps. Tuition is also offered on television channels, and information on playing casino games can often be found in your hotel room or in the playing area. Before you visit Las Vegas, the easiest way to learn is on a computer game.

On the Internet, online casinos and gaming sites also offer tuition and games to download for free, but do not be coaxed into playing games using your credit card.

Casino games

You must be over 21 years of age to gamble in Las Vegas. Visitors under this age are also prohibited from loitering in or around any area where any licensed gaming is conducted, and they cannot play, place bets or collect winnings.

Slot machines

Slot machines were originally used in Las Vegas to keep wives entertained while the men concentrated on the more serious table games. Now they make more money than any of the table games and, linked by giant networks, they offer state-wide jackpots that rise to millions of dollars.

Las Vegas has traditional slot machines, with lines of fruit or gold bars, as well as themed machines that feature stars such as Frank Sinatra or Elvis Presley, alongside television shows, classic films or board games such as Monopoly. Most casinos have machines with play ranging from 5¢ to $5, with the most popular being the 25¢, or quarter, slot machines. You often have to play more lines, or submit bigger stakes, to win the higher jackpots, but the returns on these machines are certainly generous enough to keep your attention.

Blackjack

This popular table game places the players against the dealer. Players try to get their cards to total 21, or as close to it as possible, without going over.

Each player is given two cards, usually face up, and then the dealer gives himself two cards with only one face up. When you total the cards in your hand, aces count as one or eleven, picture cards count as ten, and all others are counted at face value. When the dealer gives you the

More slot machines than you can shake a stick at!

option of more cards you can ask to be 'hit' (receive another card), or you can 'stand', if you believe that you are as close to 21 as you can get. You can be hit as many times as you like, but if you go over 21 you 'bust' and lose your bet. After each player has finished this procedure the dealer turns his second card over and tries to reach 21. If a player is closer to 21 than the dealer, he wins an amount equal to his original bet. A player who has exactly 21, or 'blackjack', receives 3–2 odds on his bet. If both the dealer and player have 21, it's known as a 'push' and nobody wins, but if the dealer busts all players win.

Craps

This exciting dice game involves the outcome of two dice, with players usually betting against the appearance of a 7. Most casinos offer tuition in this game, which is advisable for first-time players, as it appears very complicated when you watch it, but the basics are fairly simple when learned. Craps games are controlled by two dealers, who watch the bets and play; a stickman who collects the dice; and a boxman who oversees the play and personnel. As in any casino game, make sure you remember to tip the dealers, or place a bet for them, as they are often your allies in successful play.

Keno

Keno could be described as a lottery game. Nevada does not have a state lottery but keno games can be played every few minutes, in casinos, restaurants and even from your hotel room. Players choose between 1 and 15 numbers from 80 numbers on the keno form, and submit the ticket. When the game is played, a winning combination can result in some very generous winnings. Like any lottery, it is very easy to participate, but the odds are rarely in your favour.

Roulette

Often portrayed as one of the more glamorous casino games, players try to predict the outcome of the roulette wheel. As it spins, a ball races round in the opposite direction, coming to a halt in one of 38 numbered red or black slots on the wheel. When the croupier announces that players should place their bets, chips can be placed on numbers from 1 to 36, zero, or double zero. More favourable odds can be achieved, but for much smaller returns, by betting simply that the ball will land on red or black, or an odd or even number, or between a range of numbers indicated on the roulette table.

When the croupier announces there are no more bets, players wait to see where the ball settles. After the number is announced, all winning bets are paid and all other chips go to the house.

Poker

Las Vegas poker is a game of skill and certainly not for the novice. Unless you have played before and know what you are doing, it is best to leave these tables well alone. Games played in Vegas include Seven Card Stud, Texas Hold 'Em, Omaha, Omaha Hi Low, Five Card Draw and Low Ball, while house rules vary in different casinos. For beginners, the easiest way to play poker is on a video machine or in a Pai Gow poker game. However, poker is rapidly becoming very popular away from the casino and many new satellite television channels offer tips and tuition on how to master the game.

Video poker

With many variations, such as Jacks or Better, Deuces Wild and Bonus Poker, video poker can certainly be one of the most enjoyable, but addictive, machine games in Las Vegas. If you know the basic principles of poker then it's very easy to play. You are dealt five cards on the screen and then have the choice of which cards to keep and which to change. To keep cards, you can press the hold buttons below the screen, or touch the display to hold them, then the remaining cards are dealt again and winning cards are rewarded. The machines usually display the payout for each type of hand, which beginners can also use as a reference to learn the game. Expert players can play multiple hands at once.

Pai Gow poker

Not to be confused with Pai Gow, which is a game played with coloured tiles, Pai Gow poker is a card game where up to six players can play against the dealer. Like video poker, if you know the ranking of poker hands, Pai Gow poker can be a very enjoyable and relatively easy game to learn. Players are dealt seven cards, which they split into two hands, one with five cards and one with two. To win, both your hands should beat the dealer's, and if you win one each, it is regarded as 'push' or a draw. Overall, Pai Gow poker is a friendly game. The dealer can help you arrange your cards and the other players are not competing against you.

Baccarat

This game is often associated with high rollers, who have been known to bet hundreds of thousands of dollars on a single hand. However, if you find the table limit within your price range, this game is very easy to play. To win, the value of your cards must reach eight or nine. You can bet on the player or banker to win, or bet on a draw. The banker is the person that holds the shoe, which contains the playing cards and remains in their possession while the banker's hand is winning. Picture cards and tens are counted as zero, ace counts as one and other cards are taken at face value. If the total of your cards reaches two digits, the first number is ignored. For example, if you had a five and an eight, your total would be three (13, without the first digit). More cards can be drawn according to baccarat rules, and there is a small commission payable on banker bets.

Poker tables at the Horseshoe Casino

Theme parks and thrill rides

Las Vegas is the perfect city for adrenalin addicts and features some of the tallest and fastest rides in the world. Other attractions in this category give you the opportunity to relax and take in some of the magnificent sights on the Strip.

Adventuredome Theme Park

This indoor theme park has rides for all ages, but for thrill seekers try the double-loop, double-corkscrew coaster, the Canyon Blaster, the largest indoor roller coaster in the world, along with the unpredictable ride Chaos with its three ranges of motion, and the Inverter with its constant G-force, 360-degree flips and turns. In the Adventuredome the Sling Shot propels passengers up a 30m (100ft) tower at a terrifying 4G acceleration, and finally, if you want a soaking before going out into the sun, try the Rim Runner, a log ride with an 18m (60ft) drop over a waterfall.
Circus Circus Hotel & Casino, 2880 Las Vegas Blvd S.
Tel: (702) 794 3939. Open: Mon–Thur 11am–6pm, Fri–Sat 10am–midnight, Sun 10am–9pm (but with seasonal variations so check). Riders must be 1.2m (4ft) or taller to ride the Canyon Blaster, Chaos, Sling Shot, Rim Runner and Inverter. Free admission.
Charge per ride or day pass available.

Buffalo Bill's Wild West Theme Park

Located 56km (35 miles) outside Las Vegas on the California–Nevada border at Primm, Buffalo Bill's is home to the Desperado roller coaster, with its terrifying 69m (225ft) drop, and the Turbo Drop, which plummets riders 52m (170ft) downwards at 72kph (45mph) to experience negative G-force. Thrill seekers can also enjoy the programmable MaxFlight Cybercoaster and the Adventure Canyon Log Flume, among other rides.
Primm, Interstate 15 South.
Tel: (702) 382 1212. Open: Mon–Thur noon–6pm, Fri 11am–midnight, Sat 10am–midnight, Sun 10am–7pm. Riders must be at least 1.2m (4ft) for thrill rides. Admission charge.

Eiffel Tower Experience

Get a panoramic view of the city 100 storeys above the centre of the Strip.
Paris Las Vegas, 3655 Las Vegas Blvd S.
Tel: (702) 946 7000. Open: daily 9.30am–12.30am. Admission charge.

Vegas Indoor Skydiving

Try the sport of bodyflight, and experience the sensation of skydiving indoors. Freefall into a wind tunnel supported by a column of air rushing at speeds of up to 192kph (120mph).
200 Convention Center Drive.
Tel: (702) 731 4768. Open: 9.45am–8pm. Charges for flights and training packages.

Gondola rides

After walking and shopping for hours in The Venetian, relax on the Grand Canal while a singing gondolier serenades you.

The Venetian, 3355 Las Vegas Blvd S. Tel: (702) 414 1000. Open: Sun–Thur 10am–11pm, Fri & Sat 10am–midnight. Charge per ride.

The NASCAR Café

Located at the Sahara, the NASCAR Café includes the Las Vegas Cyber Speedway and Speed – the Ride. With Speedway cars seven-eighths the size of actual racing cars and mounted on hydraulic bases, experience authentic braking responses, torque and suspension on the Las Vegas Cyber Speedway. Speed – the Ride is one of the first linear-induction-motor roller coasters in the western United States, racing from 56–112kph (35–70mph) in under two seconds.

This heart-pounding ride runs underground and 69m (224ft) in the air and also races backwards.

Inside the Adventuredome Theme Park at Circus Circus

Sahara Hotel & Casino, 2535 Las Vegas Blvd S. Tel: (702) 737 2111. Café open: daily 7am–10pm. Speed – the Ride open: Sun–Thur 11am–midnight, Fri & Sat 11am–1am. The Las Vegas Cyber Speedway open: Sun–Thur 10am–midnight, Fri & Sat 10am–1am. Height restrictions apply. Charge per ride. Passes for both rides are available.

Manhattan Express

Reaching a height of 62m (203ft) and dropping 44m (144ft), this roller coaster races around the exterior of New York-New York at 107kph (67mph) and includes the breathtaking 'heart line' twist in front of the building.

New York-New York Hotel & Casino, 3790 Las Vegas Blvd S. Tel: (702) 740 6969. Open: Sun–Thur 11am–11pm, Fri & Sat 10.30am– midnight. Riders must be 1.37m (4ft 6in) or taller. Charge per ride.

SpongeBob SquarePants 4D

The hugely popular SpongeBob SquarePants steps out of the TV screens and into a 4-dimensional fun ride that sends people under the sea to Bikini Bottom pursuing a runaway pickle. Smells are one of the extra dimensions, and there are water splashes, vibrating seats and an added wind in your face to simulate fast-moving journey.

Gondolas in front of the Doge's Palace at The Venetian

The Manhattan Express winds around New York-New York

Excalibur Hotel and Casino, 3850 Las Vegas Blvd S. Tel (702) 597 7777. Open: Mon–Thur 11am–10pm, Fri 11am–11pm, Sat 10am–11pm, Sun 10am–10pm. Riders must be 1.07m (3ft 6in) or taller. Charge per ride.

Stratosphere Tower & Strat-o-Fair

On top of the tallest building west of the Mississippi are the four tallest thrill rides in the world. The Big Shot fires riders 48m (160ft) upwards from the top of the space needle. Insanity – The Ride

spins riders face down over Vegas, and X Scream propels them 8m (27ft) over the edge of the tower. The latest crazy thrill to be added to the Stratosphere is the brand new SkyJump Las Vegas. This expensive experience ($100 a time) lets you do a kind of bungee-jump from the tower using a metal cable, allowing you to fall 260m (855ft) through the air at speeds of up to 64kph (40mph).

In what must be some people's worst nightmare, you fall through the sky heading right for the Las Vegas Strip, past 108 floors of the tower, until you're brought to a stop in a controlled landing. It's the highest SkyJump in the world, and at the time of writing the only one in North America.

Stratosphere Tower Hotel & Casino, 2000 Las Vegas Blvd S.
Tel: (702) 380 7777. Open: daily 10am–1am, Fri & Sat until 2am. Height restrictions apply. Admission charge to tower with passes for rides.

Nightclubs

The first nightclub on the Strip was the Pair-O-Dice Club, which was later

Studio 54 at the MGM Grand

known as the 91 Club and owned by Police Captain Guy McAfee – who is also credited for naming the Los Angeles highway 'the Strip'. Today, there is a huge variety of nightlife to choose from, with lounge bars, hotel bars and nightclubs that open until dawn.

Dress codes apply in most nightclubs.

Blush

A small 'boutique' nightclub with plush couches and a dance floor made of onyx, Blush is a very stylish setting for conversation, dancing and even Asian appetisers.

Wynn, 3131 Las Vegas Blvd S.
Tel: (702) 770 3633. Open: Tue–Sat 9pm–late. Admission charge.

Coyote Ugly Bar & Dance Saloon

Based on the legendary bar in New York, immortalised in the film *Coyote Ugly*, female bartenders dance on the stage and encourage other women to join them. Men have to stay on the floor level, which can be pretty riotous around the bar.

New York-New York Hotel & Casino, 3790 Las Vegas Blvd S. Tel: (702) 740 6969. Open: Sun–Thur 6pm–2am, Fri–Sat 6pm–3am; Daiquiri Bar open: daily 10am–2am. Admission charge.

Ghostbar

Ghostbar is a very popular nightclub so expect long queues at the weekends, but it is worth the wait. When you reach the 55th floor, with its futuristic

interior and three glass walls, the 180-degree view is breathtaking.
Palms Casino Resort, 4321 West Flamingo Rd. Tel: (702) 938 2666. Open: nightly 8pm–4am. Admission charge.

The House of Blues

This live-music venue and nightclub has standing area and a seated balcony. Flashback Fridays offer the best of the 1970s, '80s and '90s, while Boogie Nights takes you back to the days of disco on Saturdays.
Mandalay Bay Resort & Casino, 3950 Las Vegas Blvd S. Tel: (702) 632 7777. Admission charge. Fri & Sat 11pm–early am. Special events nightly. Check current show schedules for your visit.

LAX

The new nightclub at the Luxor has 2,400sq m (26,000sq ft) of space spread over two floors, and a resident DJ.
Luxor Hotel & Casino, 3900 Las Vegas Blvd S. Tel: (702) 262 4529. Open: Wed, Fri–Sat 10pm–late. Admission charge.

Risqué de Paris

This chic after-dinner nightspot offers couches, beds and ottomans around a dance floor, as well as seven private balconies overlooking the Strip.
Paris Las Vegas, 3655 Las Vegas Blvd S. Tel: (702) 946 4589. Open: Fri & Sat 10.30pm–4am. Admission charge.

Studio 54

A high-energy nightclub on two levels, with four bars, one main dance floor and an exclusive VIP lounge. The venue is covered with memorabilia from the original Studio 54 in New York. The famous DJ Skribble hosts his 'Freak Show' on Saturdays.
MGM Grand, 3799 Las Vegas Blvd S. Tel: (702) 891 7254. www.mgmgrand.com. Open: Tue–Sat 10pm–early am. Admission charge.

Christian Audigier The Nightclub

This boutique nightclub has two DJs and a stye inspired by French fashion designer Christian Audigier.
TI, 3300 Las Vegas Blvd S. Tel: (702) 406 9723. Open: Thur–Sat 10pm–4am. Admission charge.

Wedding chapels

Join Brigitte Bardot, Joan Collins, Vic Damon, Bing Crosby, Tony Curtis and countless other celebrities who made their wedding vows Las Vegas style. Today the city is known as the wedding capital of the world, where the Clark County Marriage License Bureau states that 'All wedding parties are considered celebrities to us'.

You must obtain a licence to marry in Las Vegas (*see pp122–3 for more details*).

Hotel wedding chapels
Bellagio wedding chapels

With a choice of two beautiful chapels, the happy couple can also

What Makes Vegas Vegas

enjoy the Terrazza di Sogno, a balcony overlooking the lake and fountains.
Bellagio, 3600 Las Vegas Blvd S. Tel: (702) 693 7700. www.bellagio.com

Caesars Palace

With Roman characters and landscaping, themed or traditional weddings are available in this legendary setting.
Caesars Palace, 3570 Las Vegas Blvd S. Tel: (702) 731 7422. www.caesarspalace.com

Paris Las Vegas

This elegant hotel offers the ornate Chapelle du Paradis, the smaller Chapelle du Jardin or a poolside wedding, before the happy couple toast their future at the top of the Eiffel Tower.
Paris Las Vegas, 3655 Las Vegas Blvd S. Tel: (702) 946 7000. www.parislasvegas.com

Planet Hollywood wedding chapels

With stunning hand-painted features, the larger of these two new Mediterranean-style chapels can seat up to 60 guests. Elvis and Priscilla Presley were married in the Aladdin Hotel, which was originally on this site, so the packages include the option to have an Elvis impersonator.
Planet Hollywood, 3667 Las Vegas Blvd S. Tel: (866) 945 5933. www.planethollywood.com

Rio wedding chapels

Choose from the Palazzo Gardens, Poolside, VooDoo Lounge or the elegant ballrooms, then celebrate your wedding with a carnival theme at the Rio.
Rio All-Suite Hotel & Casino, 3700 West Flamingo Rd. Tel: (702) 777 7986. www.riolasvegas.com

The Venetian wedding chapels

Couples can choose from the resort chapel, a gondola ceremony, the Rialto Bridge, or several other romantic settings.
The Venetian Resort Hotel & Casino, 3355 Las Vegas Blvd S. Tel: (702) 414 4280. www.venetianweddings.com

Independent wedding chapels

Chapel of the Flowers

Offering three chapels within beautiful grounds, this chapel is at the north of the Strip, opposite the Stratosphere.
1717 Las Vegas Blvd S. Tel: (702) 735 4331. www.littlechapel.com

Little Church of the West

Voted best wedding chapel in Las Vegas for 16 of the last 17 years, the quaint church building is set back from the crowds on the southern tip of Las Vegas Boulevard.
4617 Las Vegas Blvd S. Tel: (702) 739 7971. www.littlechurchlv.com

Maverick Helicopters

Marry over the Strip, on Mount Charleston, at scenic Red Rock Canyon or at the bottom of the Grand Canyon. There are also packages for guests. *Maverick Helicopter Tours, 6075 Las Vegas Blvd S. Tel: (888) 261 4414. www.maverickhelicopter.com*

Wee Kirk o' the Heather

Opened in 1940, this charming venue was the first Las Vegas wedding chapel. Today it offers several different Elvis wedding packages, including Love Me Tender, Burning Love and All Shook Up. *231 Las Vegas Blvd S. Tel: (702) 382 9830. www.weekirk.com*

What Makes Vegas Vegas

Chapel of the Flowers is one of the most popular wedding venues in Las Vegas

Las Vegas weddings

Las Vegas is famed as a popular honeymoon destination where 100,000 couples get married every year. You can choose from 24-hour drive-through services, golf-club retreats, luxurious resort packages or even weddings by helicopter.

A drive-through wedding chapel

Prospective partners simply purchase a licence from the Clark County Courthouse in Las Vegas. You need to produce proof of age and ID, proof of divorce if necessary, and under-18s need written parental consent. The courthouse is open daily from 8am till midnight – it is almost too easy. With your licence in hand, almost every hotel in Las Vegas can offer you a wedding package. You can choose a French Victorian wedding service at the Monte Carlo, or enjoy a medieval service at the Canterbury Wedding Chapels at the Excalibur. You can marry by the beach at Mandalay Bay, head for the heights for a wedding in the sky at the Stratosphere Tower, or take advantage of one of the independent wedding chapels in the city.

If you want to wed away from the Strip, the Little Church of the West is located at the southern tip of Las Vegas Boulevard. Based on an old mining-town church, the chapel is the oldest structure left on the Las Vegas Strip and was the first wedding chapel in the area when it was originally located on the grounds of the Last Frontier in 1942. Its first of many celebrity weddings was the

The Little Church of the West is the oldest building on the Strip

marriage of Betty Grable and Harry James in 1943. Since then Las Vegas has become known as a wedding destination for the stars, with marriages that have included Frank Sinatra and Mia Farrow, Elvis Presley and Priscilla Beaulieu, Jane Fonda and Roger Vadim, Bruce Willis and Demi Moore, Cindy Crawford and Richard Gere, and Billy Bob Thornton and Angelina Jolie.

Another Las Vegas tradition is to have Elvis at your wedding, a service offered by many wedding chapels, such as the Graceland Chapel or Viva Las Vegas Wedding Chapel, as well as many resort chapels in the city.

THE COSTS

Weddings can range in price from a few hundred dollars to several thousands in Las Vegas, and you can preview many Las Vegas chapels on the Internet, where you can also view live weddings. Most hotels will offer wedding packages to include your honeymoon. In general, independent wedding chapels are cheaper than hotels, but allow for extra costs, which may include:

- DVD or cassette recording of your ceremony
- use of the chapel or the services of the minister
- live or recorded music
- fresh or artificial flowers
- transport

There is also a charge for the marriage licence.

Getting away from it all

Las Vegas is nestled in the southern tip of Nevada, close to the California, Utah and Arizona borders and the expansive Nellis Air Force Range to the north. This area is home to many state parks and attractions and close to the Grand Canyon National Park, while there are several other satellite cities all within a short drive of Las Vegas.

LAUGHLIN

Situated on the banks of the Colorado, this new city was founded by Don Laughlin in 1966, when he purchased a run-down motel and transformed it into the Riverside Resort Hotel and Casino. Located on the Nevada–Arizona border, 144km (90 miles) southeast of Las Vegas, Laughlin quickly flourished into a popular

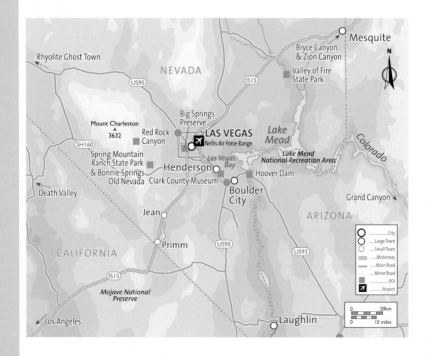

tourist destination that now attracts over five million visitors a year. There are eleven hotel casinos in Laughlin and seven golf courses in the area. You can also take to the Colorado in speedboats, on water skis in kayaks, canoes or the River Express, a river taxi that serves the waterfront casinos. Like its older cousin Las Vegas, Laughlin boasts an enviable selection of restaurants, entertainment and shopping, with the Art-Deco Horizon Outlet Center. On the other side of the Colorado lies the mining town of Oatman, still considered to be the Wild West.

Boulder City's historic district

Resort and Buffalo Bill's. The latter is also home to the famed Desperado roller coaster and the Adventure Canyon Log Flume (*see p102*).

MESQUITE

Another border town, Mesquite is located on Interstate 15, 128km (80 miles) to the northeast of Las Vegas. The city was founded in 1894, but only opened its first hotel casino in the 1980s. With four resorts, championship golf courses and award-winning spas, Mesquite is a wonderful retreat and the gateway to national parks in southern Utah, with the Zion National Park only two hours away.

PRIMM

If you drive into Las Vegas from Los Angeles on Interstate 15, Primm offers your very first glimpse of Nevada. Located on the California state line 56km (35 miles) from Las Vegas, after a long desert drive its twinkling lights tempt you with your first opportunity to gamble. There are three hotel casinos in Primm: Whisky Pete's, Primm Valley

JEAN

A little further towards Las Vegas, also on Interstate 15, is Jean, which features two themed hotels – the Gold Strike and Nevada Landing. Jean is also home to the Las Vegas Convention and Visitors Authority.

BOULDER CITY

Built to house the 5,000 workers on the Boulder Dam Project, Boulder City is one of only two cities in Nevada where gambling is illegal (the other is Panaca). Approximately 16km (10 miles) from Las Vegas, Boulder City overlooks Lake Mead and offers several recreational activities, scenic parks and a museum that details the human story behind the construction of the dam, which is only 11km (7 miles) away.

About 7km (11 miles) northwest of Boulder City, on the road from Las Vegas, stands the **Clark County**

Museum. The museum tracks the history of southern Nevada from prehistoric times to the present day, highlighting how the area around Las Vegas evolved.

1830 South Boulder Highway, Henderson. Tel: (702) 455 7955. www.co.clark.nv.us. Open: daily 9am–4.30pm. Admission charge.

THE GRAND CANYON

This awe-inspiring sight lies in the Colorado Plateau within northwest Arizona. Formed over millions of years, the Grand Canyon is a huge natural chasm 445km (277 miles) long and 1.6km (1 mile) deep. Carved by the great Colorado River, the canyon offers one of the most spectacular examples of erosion anywhere in the world. Each layer of rock provides a record of the earth's geological history and it is speculated that the rocks at the bottom of the canyon may be two billion years old.

There are many theories to explain the existence of the Canyon. The area was once a vast mountainous region – the tops have been flattened by the forces of nature, but the 1.7-billion-year-old bases of the mountains still exist. Limestone layers, such as Redwall Limestone (330 million years old) and Muav Limestone (530 million years old), provide evidence that the area was once under water, while layers like the Hermit Shale (280 million years old) contain fossils of land-based plants. Changes in the earth's orbit over

millions of years caused climatic shifts, making the water retreat and advance to create the distinctive coloured layers visible in the Canyon. Other geological factors, such as continental drift and the subsequent volcanic and seismic activity, also played a huge role in the Canyon's formation and created the younger rock formations found in the Bryce and Zion canyons. Then 60–70 million years ago the Rocky Mountains were formed, and the Colorado River began its flow. When the Colorado Plateau began to lift upwards, the river changed course and started to carve out the Grand Canyon, exposing the geological history of the area.

Tours

Several tour operators offer trips to the Grand Canyon. Most popular are the flight tours from Las Vegas, lasting from a few hours to a whole day. You can fly down early in the morning, see the sunrise and stop for brunch on the edge of the canyon, then return before midday. Alternatively, you can spend a whole day in the park, visit Indian reservations and see the sun set.

The two main visitor areas are the North and South Rims of the Canyon, which offer breathtaking vistas of raised plateaus and steep-walled canyons, stunning views that will far outrival any other natural formation of this kind. By car, the South Rim (where the visitor centre is located) is approximately 432km (270 miles) from Las Vegas, while the North Rim is *c.* 416km

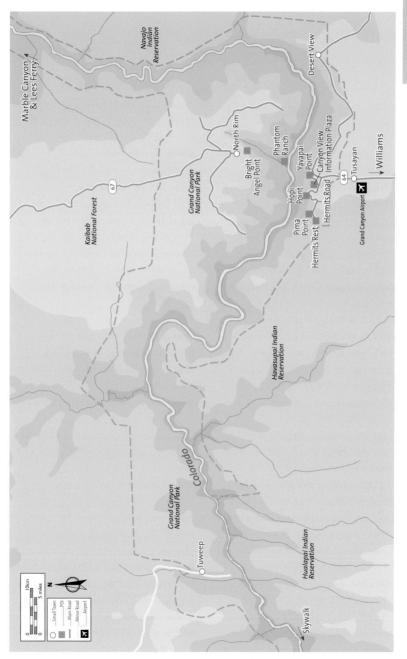

Getting away from it all

Navajo Indian Reservation

Marble Canyon & Lees Ferry

Kaibab National Forest

Grand Canyon National Park

67

North Rim

Bright Angel Point

Phantom Ranch

Yavapai Point

Hopi Point

Pima Point

Hermits Rest

Hermits Road

Canyon View Information Plaza

Desert View

64

Tusayan

Williams

Grand Canyon Airport

Havasupai Indian Reservation

Colorado

Grand Canyon National Park

Tuweep

Hualapai Indian Reservation

Skywalk

N

0   10km
0   5 miles

Small Town
POI
Main Road
Minor Road
Airport

Helicopter tours are a popular way to see the Grand Canyon

(260 miles). Across the canyon the two rims are only 16km (10 miles) away from each other, but by road they are separated by *c.* 344km (215 miles).

For hikers, the canyon provides over 640km (400 miles) of trails, and there are many camping and lodge facilities available. It's advisable to make reservations early, particularly on the South Rim where activities and lodgings can be booked well in advance. Both of the rims are at a very high altitude so all activity will be strenuous, even walking.

South of the Colorado lies the Havasupai Indian Reservation, which can only by reached by horseback or a 13km (8-mile) hike, while the Hualapai Indian Reservation is further west.

Wildlife

The Grand Canyon supports many rare plant and animal species, some of which are unique to the area. Its ecosystem creates an environment as diverse as the area stretching between Canada and Mexico, as the canyon provides five out of seven life zones identified in the United States: the Lower Sonoran, Upper Sonoran, Transition, Canadian and Hudsonian.

The Grand Canyon is home to over 1,500 plant species, along with 355 birds, 89 mammals, 47 reptiles, 9 amphibians and 17 species of fish. Highlights include the endangered humpbacked chub, found only in the Colorado River system, and the largest land bird in America, the California condor, a member of the vulture family. Other birds and mammals include owls, hummingbirds, woodpeckers, bats, squirrels, bighorn sheep, mountain lions, wild burros, porcupines and skunks.

It is illegal to feed or approach wild animals, especially deer and squirrels, as this threatens their environment and they may become addicted to human food. Avoid all wild animals: deer can kick and squirrels often bite eager tourists. The park imposes fines of up to $5,000 for anyone caught feeding or disturbing the animals, and if you see anyone breaking these rules, advise them to stop, or notify the park authorities.

Climate

In the summer, temperatures at the South Rim are generally 10–26°C (50–80°F), while in the winter ice may affect the roads or trails and there will be some closures due to snow. Temperatures at these times can range from –1 to –18°C (30–0°F). During the spring and autumn the weather can be very changeable, so check weather forecasts when you plan your visit.

At a slightly higher elevation than the South Rim, temperatures at the North Rim are a little cooler. Highway 67, leading to the North Rim, is closed during the winter. Snow can also appear at any time of year on this rim. Both rims are prone to afternoon rain.

In the summer, the inner canyon can be extremely hot and, as you descend, the temperature rises. It can reach over 49°C (120°F) by the river.

The South Rim

With an elevation of *c.* 2,100m (7,000ft) above sea level, the South Rim of the canyon is *c.* 432km (270 miles) from Las Vegas by car. The Grand Canyon National Park attracts over five million visitors every year, so prepare for this popular lookout point to be very busy in the summer months. Quieter times to visit would be from November to February, but winter weather may affect your visit.

The Canyon View Information Plaza, which is also the park headquarters, offers a bookshop, visitor centre and toilet facilities, by Yavapai Point. There are several points to view the canyon and look down towards the Colorado to the east and west of the rim, such as Hermit's Rest, 13km (8 miles) to the west of the centre, which takes in Hopi and Pima Point. Known as Hermit's Road, this route is usually closed to private vehicles, but a shuttle bus can take you to some of the viewpoints and the route can also be walked. Some sections are paved, but often run close to the rim and can be narrow in places. Cycling along this route is not allowed.

SAFETY

When visiting the Grand Canyon, follow safety guidelines issued by the park authorities.

- Stay on the trails and avoid the edges. Only take vehicles and bicycles on maintained roads for private vehicles.
- Avoid visiting during thunderstorms.
- Wear suncream and protective clothing, and ensure you have plenty of water.
- Be aware that the altitude will be physically demanding.

Over 250 hikers have to be rescued every year, usually due to exhaustion or dehydration. Hikers should rest, stay in the shade, drink plenty of water and wear protective clothing. Do not attempt to reach the river and return in one day.

To the east of the visitor centre is Desert View Drive, which you can access by car. It follows the canyon rim for 42km (26 miles) past overlooks such as Yaki Point, Grandview Point, Moran Point and Lipan Point just before it reaches Desert View, which has camping and food services.

The Grand Canyon Village offers food, camping and lodging facilities and the area is also served by the Grand Canyon Airport in Tusayan, which offers more facilities, and shuttles to the rim.

The North Rim

Located 416km (260 miles) from Las Vegas, the North Rim is only open from mid-May until mid-October. There is a shuttle service from the South Rim, but this journey is over 344km (215 miles). Driving in on Highway 67, the entrance to the Rim and the Grand Canyon Lodge is close to Bright Angel Point, where you can look over Angel Canyon and catch a glimpse of the South Rim. The North Rim is approximately 2,400m (8,000ft) above sea level, so the altitude can be very demanding. You tend to look over and across the canyon rather than into it, and along with the Grand Canyon Lodge area, the main lookouts include Point Imperial, where at 2,683m (8,803ft) you can see the canyon evolve from the narrow Marble Canyon to the expanse of the Grand Canyon. Beyond this, Cape Royal is a popular place to watch the sunrise and sunset and see the Colorado arch gracefully into the canyon, while Point

GRAND CANYON SKYWALK

One of the newest and most unusual ways to view the Grand Canyon is from the **Skywalk**, a glass walkway jutting out over a side canyon. It extends some 20m (66ft) beyond the edge, and is approximately 1,220m (4,000ft) above the canyon floor. With just 10cm (4in) of glass between you and the fresh air below, it's not for the faint-hearted! *Grand Canyon Skywalk, Grand Canyon West. Tel: (877) 716 9378. www.grandcanyonskywalk.com. Admission charge.*

Sublime offers a fantastic view, although you will need a 4WD vehicle to reach it.

How to get there
The South Rim
By car, drive southeast on US 93 past the Hoover Dam to SR 40 east to Williams, then take the 64 and 180 north to the Grand Canyon Village.

The North Rim
Drive east on Interstate 15 to SR 9 (north of St George, Utah), continue to go east, then take SR 89 south on Mount Carmel junction leading to the North Rim.

Tours
You can reach the Grand Canyon in one hour by plane or helicopter, and there are countless tours available from Las Vegas, including:

American Adventure Tours, with a huge selection of tours, including the North and South Rim and Colorado

Raft Tours. *Tel: (702) 876 4600. www.americanadventuretours.com.*
Maverick Helicopter Tours, with private landing areas in the Canyon. *6075 Las Vegas Blvd S. Tel: (888) 261 4414. www.maverickhelicopter.com*

Backcountry and the Colorado

Hiking down to the river can be described as either exhilarating or an ordeal. Heading downwards in a desert environment, hikers face steep descents and rising temperatures. Then on their return they have strenuous climbs. The Grand Canyon covers over 0.5 million hectares (1.2 million acres) and includes 640km (400 miles) of hiking trails. It is not safe to try to hike to the bottom of the canyon and return in one day, so you will have to obtain a permit to stay overnight. Permits need to be applied for a year in advance and spaces are limited. The park authorities want the minimum of human impact in the area and there are strict guidelines to follow.

The only place you can cross the Colorado River is at Phantom Ranch, below both the North and South Rims. To reach the river by car, you will need to drive to Lees Ferry near Marble Canyon. Activities on the Colorado include sightseeing tours and private river trips, ranging from one day on the water to a trip lasting several days. White-water rafting is also available.

TUWEEP

With a drop of 900m (3,000ft) into the canyon, Tuweep is located on the north side of the Colorado and its lava flows and cinder columns offer evidence of the volcanic activity that once took place here. Camping is available but the road to Tuweep is unpaved.

The North Rim of the Grand Canyon

Twentieth-century marvel

The Hoover Dam is one of America's seven Modern Civil Engineering wonders. Just 48km (30 miles) outside Las Vegas, the dam meets the domestic water needs of over 18 million people in Nevada, Arizona and California and also generates low-cost hydroelectric power for the same three states.

The dam is fuelled by the great Colorado River, which runs a 2,240km (1,400-mile) course from the Colorado Rocky Mountains to the Gulf of California. During the 1800s and early 1900s, the river often flooded, destroying millions of dollars' worth of crops, so a determined effort had to be made to control its flow and harness the resources it could provide.

In 1922 the Colorado River Compact divided the river among the seven states it ran through, paving the way for a series of storage dams. Six years later, President Calvin Coolidge signed the Boulder Dam Project Act, and then construction began in 1931. After a previous site was found to be unsuitable, engineers settled on Black Canyon and the dam began to take shape.

A record 2.37 million cu m (3.25 million cu yd) of concrete was poured over a four-year period, completing the dam well within budget and two years ahead of schedule. It was the most ambitious engineering project since the construction of the Panama Canal in the early 1900s and provided work for an influx of new residents who signed up for the project as the country recovered from the Great Depression. As gambling was legalised in Nevada, the city of Las Vegas boomed with the dam's construction, although the project management soon put paid to any

The Hoover Dam and Lake Mead beyond

Memorial to those who died constructing the dam

free spending. Workers were housed in rows of tents, creating the fledgling town known as Boulder City where drinking and gambling were prohibited. Las Vegas was reserved for the weekend.

Working in harsh desert conditions, many lives were lost during completion of the dam. It was finally dedicated on 30 September 1935 by President Franklin D Roosevelt as millions tuned in to the radio to hear him proclaim it a '20th-century marvel'. Then, as the dam held back the mighty Colorado, it created Lake Mead, America's largest man-made reservoir, named after Reclamation Commissioner Dr Elwood Mead. The lake can store 9.2 trillion US gallons of water, which is drawn into the dam by intake towers and flows through penstocks to the power plant. The first generator was installed in 1936, followed by a further 16 to generate more than four billion kilowatt hours of electricity per year.

Herbert Hoover, the 31st US president, became one of the greatest supporters of the project, and in 1947 the Boulder Dam was officially renamed Hoover Dam in his honour. He believed that the dam should be self-financed through the sale of electricity, and by this method the $165-million cost of the project was repaid.

As a National Historic Landmark, Hoover Dam is open to the public and it is visited by almost ten million people every year.
Visitor Center: open 9am–6pm.
Tickets for tours are only sold on the day, on a first-come first-served basis.

THE HOOVER DAM AND LAKE MEAD

The Hoover Dam and Lake Mead are two breathtaking sights located just a short drive away from Las Vegas. Both man-made creations, the Hoover Dam was constructed to harness the great Colorado River, while Lake Mead rose from the backed-up water that headed south from the Rocky Mountains.

Hoover Dam

Open all year round, you can drive or walk over the great arch of the Hoover Dam, which is located southeast of Las Vegas on the Nevada–Arizona border. It is forbidden to stop your car on the dam, situated on US Highway 93, but there are parking facilities at the Hoover Dam Visitor Center. The Powerplant Tour currently costs $11 for adults, while the full Hoover Dam Tour is $30. The busiest times to visit are during the summer months and over Easter. Arrive early in the day to avoid the heat and the crowds.

Lake Mead

The largest man-made reservoir in the United States, Lake Mead offers an impressive 880km (550 miles) of shoreline and has a storage capacity of 3.5 billion cu m (9,299,792,116,392 US gallons). In 1964 it was proclaimed the first National Recreation Area, and it offers watersports such as swimming, boating and fishing, sightseeing activities, lodging, camping and simply sunbathing. Diverse ecosystems from the Mojave Desert, the Great Basin and the Sonoran Deserts all intersect at Lake Mead, providing resources for wildlife education and conservation.

Approximately 40km (25 miles) from Las Vegas at its closest point, Lake Mead is open all year round and can easily be reached off the Boulder Highway on Route 93. Areas such as Las Vegas Bay, Lake Mead Marina and Boulder Beach feature restaurants, marinas, sporting activities and sightseeing cruises, particularly at Boulder Beach, which is closer to the dam. There are also several islands such as Black Island and the Boulder Islands within the lake, which stretches far over the border into Arizona. The Alan Bible Visitor Center is located off US

Hoover Dam, *US Route 93, Boulder City. Tel: (702) 494 2517. Visitor centre open: daily (except for Thanksgiving and Christmas) 9am–6pm. Parking garage open: 8am–5.45pm. Admission is $8 (tours extra and there is an additional parking fee).*
Food and drink are not allowed on the tour but water bottles can be carried. The Hoover Dam Visitor Center and the Hoover Dam Discovery Tour are accessible for wheelchairs.

Lake Mead National Recreation Area, *601 Nevada Highway, Boulder City. Tel: (702) 293 8907/(702) 293 8990 (weekends). Lake Mead is open all year round, 24 hours a day. Visitor centre open: daily (except Thanksgiving, Christmas and New Year's Day) 8.30am–4.30pm.*

Highway 93, near Boulder City, and other visitor centres are situated at Overton Beach, Echo Bay, Callville Bay, Las Vegas Bay and Temple Bar in Arizona.

Around the crystal-blue waters of Lake Mead may be found several lodging and camping facilities, all set against an impressive backdrop of ridges, mountains and desert.

The massive concrete walls of the Hoover Dam

OTHER EXCURSIONS

While Las Vegas is a creation of the 20th century, located just a few miles outside the city are many national parks offering breathtaking geological formations and scenery. From imposing rock formations to the depths of the canyons, the area around Las Vegas offers a rich diversity of landscapes.

Mount Charleston

Located 56km (35 miles) northwest of Las Vegas, in the Toiyabe National Forest, Mount Charleston rises to around 3,632m (11,918ft). Visitors can enjoy horseriding, cycling and hiking, while winter activities include skiing, snowboarding and sleigh rides. There are hotels available all year round and camping facilities from May to September. The temperatures at Mount Charleston can be much lower than in Las Vegas, so although it may be a welcome break from the heat, make sure you take suitable clothing. From Las Vegas, you can reach Mount Charleston from Kyle Canyon, State Highway 157, northwest of the city off Route 95.
Tel: (702) 873 8800, or ask at your hotel desk for travel information.

Red Rock Canyon

With its stunning rock formations, Red Rock Canyon is popular for anyone with a passion for exploring. For those with an adventurous spirit there are cliffs, sheer drops and hidden crevices, along with a paved 21km (13-mile) loop drive for those who want to take things a little easier. The scenery is outstanding, thanks to the Keystone Thrust Fault, which has forced ancient grey rocks over the top of newer red sandstone. The red-blazoned rocks are complemented by sweeping sand dunes in an area which is also home to wild burros, bighorn sheep, wild horses and coyotes.

Famed for its rock-climbing opportunities, other recreational activities available include cycling, climbing and hiking. There are also sites of geological and historical interest, along with a museum and visitor centre.

Only 24km (15 miles) west of Las Vegas, the Red Rock Canyon National Conservation Area can be reached from Charleston Boulevard, which meets State Highway 159 to the west of Las Vegas; the road then loops around the side of the canyon area to join the 160 back into the city.
Tel: (661) 320 4001, or ask at your hotel desk for travel information.
Open: daily 6am–8pm in summer

RHYOLITE GHOST TOWN

If you drive through the desert by car, you will see a few signs leading you to ghost towns such as **Rhyolite**, which is described as the Gateway to Death Valley. Located near to Beatty Nevada, 192km (120 miles) north of Las Vegas, Rhyolite includes ruins of the general store, banks, a school, railroad depot and a house made entirely from glass bottles.

(closes at 5pm in winter). There are guided hikes on Sat & Sun 9am.

Death Valley

Located in western California, Death Valley National Park, at 85m (280ft) below sea level, is the lowest point in the Northern Hemisphere. This 250km (155-mile) trench runs between the Amargosa mountain range to the east and the Panamint range to the west. The highest point in the range is Telescope Peak at 3,368m (11,049ft), only 24km (15 miles) from the lowest point of Badwater Basin salt pan. Death Valley is 216km (135 miles) west of Las Vegas, and you can see many examples of the earth's diverse geological eras. Its harsh desert environment creates unique plant and animal species but the heat can be intense. Although the area seems far too inhospitable for human life, archaeologists have found evidence of

The desolate sand dunes and multicoloured rock of Death Valley

Getting away from it all

An ancient petroglyph in the Valley of Fire

miners, prospectors and settlers, while Native Americans still reside in the area today.
Tel: (760) 786 3200. www.nps.gov/deva

Valley of Fire State Park

The Valley of Fire State Park is 88km (55 miles) northeast of Las Vegas, on State Highway 176, off Interstate 15. Mysterious petroglyphs, or rock carvings, provide evidence of ancient Native American civilisations hidden within the beautiful canyon landscape with its red rock formations. The Valley of Fire State Park is close to Overton, home of the **Lost City Museum**, which provides a fascinating insight into the Anasazi, or 'Ancient ones', who lived in the valley centuries ago.

The Nevada Park Service runs a visitor centre in the Valley of Fire State Park and tours are also available. The park is open to visitors all year round.

Bryce Canyon

With unique rock formations such as the Pink Cliffs, Silent City and the Cathedral, Bryce Canyon is a magnificent sight located 336km (210 miles) northeast of Las Vegas, in southwestern Utah.
Tel: (435) 834 5322. www.nps.gov/brca

Mojave National Preserve

The Mojave National Preserve is a 0.64-million-hectare (1.6-million-acre) park with volcanic cinder cones, Joshua tree forests, sand dunes and mountains. Located 96km (60 miles) southwest of Las Vegas, the visitor centres are in Baker and Needles, California.
Tel: (760) 252 6108. www.nps.gov/moja

Spring Mountain Ranch State Park

This ranch was once owned by billionaire Howard Hughes and was originally a resting point for travellers on the Mormon and Spanish trails. Located 48km (30 miles) west of Las Vegas, the park is open all year round and offers outdoor theatre performances as well as jazz concerts.
Tel: (775) 875 4141.
www.parks.nv.gov/smr.htm

Zion Canyon

Zion National Park is situated in Utah, at the junction of the Colorado Plateau, Great Basin and the Mojave Desert, 253km (158 miles) north of Las Vegas on Interstate 15. Hebrew in origin, the name Zion describes the area as a place

of sanctuary – and with its majestic rock formations, forest plateaus and vast desert areas, the park certainly gives you the opportunity to see Mother Nature at her best. The Zion Canyon is formed by the Virgin River carving its way through the sandstone to create canyon walls up to 900m (3,000ft) high, while at the same time creating lush greenery along its flow. *Tel: (435) 772 3256.*
www.nps.gov/zion

LOS ANGELES

Certainly not a wonder of nature, but the city of Los Angeles, like Las Vegas, made its mark in the 20th century. By car, you can reach Los Angeles in five to six hours and it is worthwhile taking a couple of days out to visit Disneyland® and Universal Studios, see the stars on Hollywood Boulevard or drive past the homes of the rich and famous in Beverly Hills. Plan your trip carefully, as the roads are known for their congestion and Los Angeles is a vast city that can be quite difficult to navigate.

Getting away from it all

Zion National Park, a place of tranquillity

The Wild West

Nevada is home to several Native American tribes, such as the Washo, Shoshone, Gosha and Paiute. The earliest known settlers were the Anasazi, or 'Ancient ones', with the only clues to their existence being offered in rock carvings known as petroglyphs.

North Nevada is famed as cowboy territory, and references to the Wild West can be found throughout the state. In its early years as a tourist destination, Las Vegas housed a collection of Western saloons and dude ranches, where guests could ride horses and play the part of a cowboy for a couple of weeks. The first Downtown establishments had wooden sawdust-covered floors, and the same Western theme was carried on with the first buildings on the Strip. Starting with the railroads in the late 19th century, America was going through some great changes. In the 1930s and '40s, after World War I and the hardships of the Great Depression, and in the midst of a new conflict, resorts such as El Rancho and the Last Frontier offered a last chance to hold on to the Old West.

Bonnie Springs Old Nevada, originally built in 1843 on the old Spanish trail

Today, visitors to Nevada can still visit dude ranches. If you want to work a little harder, you can drive cattle and round up horses by staying on a working ranch, while adept horse riders can take part in exhilarating horse drives. Many side trips from Las Vegas take in cowboy ranches or Indian reservations, and they are often offered as part of coach and helicopter tours to the Grand Canyon.

Just 45 minutes from the Strip, **Bonnie Springs Old Nevada** was a frequent resting point for travellers on the old Spanish trail to California. Now, in this Wild West theme park, visitors can witness dramatic action that includes gunfights and hangings, in an old town that features a post office, blacksmith display, various old stores and the Boot Hill cemetery. This is a great attraction for children, who can also enjoy the petting zoo and rides. *(Tel: (702) 875 4191. www.bonniesprings.com. Open: Wed–Sun 10.30am–6pm (summer), Wed–Fri 11am–5pm, Sat & Sun 10.30am–5pm (winter). Admission charge.)*

There are several Native American reservations around the Las Vegas area. You can take part in a pow wow, a traditional get-together where tribes gather to exchange gifts, sell food and crafts, and hear the news. These festive meetings include tribal dances and rodeos, such as the Snow

Bonnie Springs Old Nevada

Mountain Pow Wow, which is held by the Las Vegas Colony, northwest of the city, on Memorial Day weekend in May.

Northeast of Las Vegas is the Moapa Indian Reservation, known for its duty-free tobacco and fireworks, although the latter are prohibited outside the reservation area. Another reservation, Fort Mojave, is just south of the Laughlin area.

East of Las Vegas on Interstate 15 is the Lost City Museum in Overton, with Anasazi artefacts and reconstructed pit dwellings. The Anasazi lived in the Moapa Valley from the 1st to the 12th century, close to the Valley of Fire State Park, where petroglyphs and stunning rock formations can be found (*see p126*).

Accommodation

In general, room rates in Las Vegas are extremely reasonable, and you pay one price for the room rather than for each person. For the best prices contact the hotels directly, through their booking line, or visit their websites. Rates are higher at the weekend so, for the best prices, incorporate as many weekdays as you can. Standard rooms usually include one king-size bed or two queen beds, which you can choose when booking.

Price guide, per room:

★   Under $50
★★ $50–$100
★★★ $101–$200
★★★★   Over $200

These prices are based on low-season midweek prices for a standard room.

Strip hotels and resorts

Compared with other cities, Las Vegas Strip resorts offer some of the most luxurious hotel rooms for extremely competitive prices.

California Hotel ★

Not to be confused with the Eagles' Hotel California, this is a mix of California and Hawaii, which is where most of the guests come from. Expect to find Hawaiian food and Hawaiian shirts, and while it doesn't quite have the range of facilities that other properties have, it's inexpensive and great value if you're on a budget.
12 East Ogden Ave. Tel: (702) 385 1222. www.thecal.com

Circus Circus Hotel & Casino ★

One of the most family-friendly resorts on the Strip, with over 3,700 rooms; the carnival theme continues in the rooms.
2880 Las Vegas Blvd S.
Tel: (702) 734 0410.
www.circuscircus.com

Sahara Hotel & Casino ★

Featuring 1,720 recently refurbished guest rooms with a Moroccan theme, the Sahara is at the north end of the Strip.
2535 Las Vegas Blvd S.
Tel: (702) 737 2111.
www.saharavegas.com

Bally's Las Vegas ★★

This elegant resort with moving walkways to its entrance is located in the centre of the Strip. Guest towers include Parlor suites and standard rooms.
3645 Las Vegas Blvd S.
Tel: (702) 739 4111. www.ballyslv.com

Excalibur Hotel & Casino ★★
Resembling a medieval castle, the Excalibur resort at the south end of the Strip is another family favourite with a large pool complex.
3850 Las Vegas Blvd S.
Tel: (702) 597 7777. www.excalibur.com

Flamingo Las Vegas ★★
A favourite for regular visitors, with 3,500 rooms, this resort features beautiful lagoons and swimming areas (*see pp44–5*).
3555 Las Vegas Blvd S.
Tel: (702) 733 3111.
www.flamingolasvegas.com

Imperial Palace Hotel & Casino ★★
Themed on the Orient, rooms include Standard, Penthouse and King suites.
3535 Las Vegas Blvd S. Tel: (702) 731 3311. www.imperialpalace.com

Luxor Hotel & Casino ★★
This popular family resort towards the south of the Strip has 4,400 rooms, all designed with an Egyptian theme.
2830 Las Vegas Blvd S.
Tel: (702) 262 4000. www.luxor.com

Monte Carlo Resort & Casino ★★
Always maintaining a European elegance and not only in the glamorous

Opened in 1993, the Luxor now has 4,400 rooms

casino, the Monte Carlo offers over 3,000 de luxe rooms and suites.
3770 Las Vegas Blvd S. Tel: (702) 730 7777. www.montecarlo.com

New York-New York Hotel & Casino ★★

The 2,000 guest rooms in this stunning resort are located in skyscraper towers that re-create the Manhattan skyline (*see pp34–5*).
3790 Las Vegas Blvd S. Tel: (702) 740 6969. www.nynyhotelcasino.com

The ARIA opened in December 2009

ARIA Resort & Casino at CityCenter ★★★

This 61-storey super-modern hotel in the new CityCenter project has over 4,000 rooms, 16 restaurants and the latest Cirque du Soleil show *Viva ELVIS* as just some of its features.
3730 Las Vegas Blvd S. Tel: (866) 359 7111. www.arialasvegas.com

Caesars Palace ★★★

A luxurious resort located in the centre of the Strip with some of the finest European-style hotel rooms in Las Vegas (*see pp40–41*).
3570 Las Vegas Blvd S. Tel: (702) 731 7110. www.caesarspalace.com

Encore Las Vegas ★★★

Steve Wynn's encore after building Wynn Las Vegas is, naturally, named Encore Las Vegas. It's yet another attempt to raise the bar on just how luxurious a Vegas hotel can be, and it certainly has one of the best spas in the city, with 6,500sq m (70,000sq ft) of sumptuousness.
3131 Las Vegas Blvd S. Tel: (702) 770 7171. www.encorelasvegas.com

Harrah's ★★★

Harrah's has been around since the 1970s and despite some major renovations in the last few years, it still has that old-fashioned Vegas feel – which is what a lot of people want. Comedian Rita Rudner is the headliner, and Mac King's Magic Show has been voted Best Afternoon Show in Vegas.

3475 Las Vegas Blvd S. Tel: (800) 214 9110. www.harrahslasvegas.com

Mandalay Bay Resort & Casino ★★★
This South Seas paradise features a luxurious swimming area and bay, and more than 3,200 spacious rooms and suites.
3950 Las Vegas Blvd S. Tel: (702) 632 7777. www.mandalaybay.com

MGM Grand Hotel & Casino ★★★
This is one of the largest hotels in the world and is located on the south end of the Strip with over 5,000 guest rooms.
3799 Las Vegas Blvd S. Tel: (702) 891 7777. www.mgmgrand.com

Mirage ★★★
This tropical paradise with its own fiery volcano offers nearly 3,000 de luxe rooms and suites and is located right in the centre of the Strip.
3400 Las Vegas Blvd S. Tel: (702) 791 7111. www.mirage.com

Paris Las Vegas ★★★
This romantic resort in the centre of the Strip features 3,000 beautiful hotel rooms with luxurious custom-designed furnishings.
3655 Las Vegas Blvd S. Tel: (800) 946 7000. www.parislasvegas.com

**The Venetian Resort
Hotel & Casino** ★★★
With over 4,000 suites, the rooms at The Venetian are twice the size of

standard Vegas rooms, with features such as sunken lounges and canopy-draped king-size beds (*see pp49–51*).
3355 Las Vegas Blvd S. Tel: (702) 414 1000. www.venetian.com

Bellagio ★★★★
This AAA Five Diamond award-winning resort overlooks the fountains of Bellagio in the centre of the Strip and features nearly 4,000 opulent guest rooms and suites (*see pp38–40*).
3600 Las Vegas Blvd S. Tel: (702) 693 7111. www.bellagio.com

Four Seasons ★★★★
A calm oasis, located on the upper-level floors of the Mandalay Bay hotel. The 338 spacious rooms and 86 suites with their floor-to-ceiling windows are a paradigm of hotel-room elegance, while the 'secret' passageway that leads to the Mandalay casino is just a part of the Four Seasons' emphasis on discretion, or unashamed exclusivity and elitism.
3960 Las Vegas Blvd S. Tel: (702) 632 5000. www.fourseasons.com

Mandarin Oriental ★★★★
By Vegas standards, the new Mandarin Oriental is boutique-sized, with just 392 rooms and suites. It's located in the CityCenter and oozes luxury, in typical Mandarin style. Renowned French chef Pierre Gagnaire has been brought in to oversee their 23rd-floor restaurant, with its stunning Vegas views, while the spa has a touch of 1930s Shanghai about it. Definitely

different, and not cheap, but worth the splurge.
3752 Las Vegas Boulevard S.
Tel: (702) 590 8888.
www.mandarinoriental.com/lasvegas

Planet Hollywood Resort & Casino ★★★★

Formerly the Aladdin Hotel and Casino, this flagship hotel of the Planet Hollywood chain has almost 2,500 rooms and apartments decorated with film memorabilia, plus a selection of restaurants. It is centrally located on the Las Vegas Strip.
3667 Las Vegas Blvd S.
Tel: (877) 333 9474.
www.planethollywoodresort.com

Wynn Las Vegas ★★★★

The Wynn raised the stakes for Las Vegas luxury when it opened in 2005. The rooms are decorated like the galleries of a museum, the casino even defies the customary tack and tastelessness of its peers, and the swimming pools and golf course are nothing short of breathtaking.
3131 Las Vegas Blvd S.
Tel: (702) 770 7100.
www.wynnlasvegas.com

Off-Strip hotels

Resort prices can be a lot cheaper off the Strip, but offer the same standard of accommodation and service. There are also many popular chains in the city, such as Budget Suites, Hampton Inn and Holiday Inn.

Gold Coast Hotel & Casino ★

This 711-room hotel is one mile east of the Strip but provides a free shuttle bus back and forth, and its location also means free car parking, which, on top of the amazingly cheap rooms, means it's a great bargain. It has a good range of cafés and restaurants, some reflecting its proximity to Vegas's Chinatown, and a modest entertainment schedule too.
4000 West Flamingo Rd.
Tel: (702) 367 7111.
www.goldcoastcasino.com

Las Vegas Hilton ★

Highly recommended, this friendly luxurious resort was once the largest hotel in the world, with 3,000 rooms, but is the largest Hilton in the world.
3000 Paradise Rd. Tel: (702) 732 5111.
www.lvhilton.com

The Orleans Hotel & Casino ★

A Mardi Gras-themed hotel, with over 1,800 rooms, the Orleans is just off the south end of the Strip and also offers a 70-lane bowling alley.
4500 Tropicana Ave.
Tel: (702) 365 7111.
www.orleanscasino.com

Vegas Club Hotel & Casino ★

Aim to get one of the rooms that has a view of the *Fremont Street Experience* in this dirt cheap but good quality 400-room hotel. The Vegas Club has a sporting theme, which of course means more to US visitors than

The 3,000-room Las Vegas Hilton

those from overseas, but it's a fun place, with a range of restaurants and access to some of the facilities at its sister property, the Plaza, including the rooftop pool.
18 Fremont St. Tel: (702) 385 1664. vegasclubcasino.net

Four Queens ★★
Cheap rates in a hotel that dates from 1966 and that has retained its old-style

Vegas glitz. With 690 rooms and only three restaurants, it can't compete in the entertainment stakes, but the focus here is on the casino and it does offer a good deal for those wanting to gamble.
202 Fremont St. Tel: (702) 385 4011. www.fourqueens.com

Golden Nugget ★★
In the heart of Fremont Street, this ornate hotel features nearly 2,000 guest

Ipanema Beach at Rio

rooms and was refurbished by developer Steve Wynn (famed for the Bellagio and the Wynn).
129 East Fremont St. Tel: (702) 385 7111. www.goldennugget.com

Hooters Casino Hotel ★★

It's surprising that it's taken Hooters so long to open a hotel in Vegas, as they fit in so naturally here. The Hooters hotel experience is very like the Hooters bar chain experience – girls in tight T-shirts and even tighter hot pants are everywhere – but it's an excellently run and designed Vegas casino hotel.
115 East Tropicana Ave.

Tel: (702) 739 9000.
www.hooterscasinohotel.com

Main Street Station ★★

This hotel, casino and brewery is close to Fremont Street and is one of the best choices Downtown if you want cheap room rates but good facilities. There's a free shuttle service to the Strip, over 400 rooms, 3 restaurants including the excellent Triple 7 Restaurant and Microbrewery, and a decent casino too.
200 North Main St.
Tel: (702) 387 1896.
www.mainstreetcasino.com

Palms Casino Resort ★★

This adult-themed resort with 1,600 guest rooms includes dance poles and dance floors in its Playpen suites.
4321 West Flamingo Rd.
Tel: (702) 942 7777. www.palms.com

Hard Rock Hotel & Casino ★★★

This rock 'n' roll paradise is located only one road east of the Strip. It offers 657 guest rooms and luxury suites and attracts a fun-loving crowd.
4455 Paradise Rd. Tel: (702) 693 5000.
www.hardrockhotel.com

J W Marriott Resort & Spa ★★★

Located in the upscale neighbourhood of Summerlin, some 16km (10 miles) from the Strip, this stunning resort caters to every whim, with its stylish rooms, an indulgent spa and a serene 'off-the-Strip' location.
221 North Rampart Blvd.
Tel: (702) 869 7777.
www.jwlasvegasresort.com

Red Rock Casino Resort & Spa ★★★

This new resort in Summerlin provides luxurious contemporary rooms with Martini bars and even LCD TVs in the bathrooms. Rande Gerber's on-site nightclub draws celebrities and aspirational hipsters, but the major lure is the resort's breathtaking mountain setting.
11011 West Charleston Blvd.
Tel: (702) 797 7777.
www.redrocklasvegas.com

Rio All-Suite Hotel & Casino ★★★

With 2,500 suites, all with fridges and floor-to-ceiling windows offering fantastic views, this Brazilian-themed resort is highly recommended.
3700 West Flamingo Rd.
Tel: (702) 252 7777. www.playrio.com

Westin Casuarina Hotel, Casino & Spa ★★★

A calm sanctuary just one block east of the Strip, the Westin provides comfortable, if rather small, rooms.
160 East Flamingo Rd.
Tel: (702) 836 9775.
www.starwoodhotels.com/westin

Loews Lake Las Vegas Resort ★★★★

Sumptuous accommodation nestling on the shores of the resort's private 130-hectare (320-acre) lake. An ideal base to explore the region and enjoy the many recreational sports offered on-site, including golf, kayaking, fishing and windsurfing.
1600 Lake Las Vegas Pkwy, Henderson.
Tel: (702) 564 1600.

Platinum Hotel & Spa ★★★★

East of the Strip, the Platinum represents the new breed of Las Vegas hotel that focuses on lifestyle pursuits and relaxation over gambling. Each suite includes a gourmet kitchen, living room and whirlpool baths. The attractions of the Strip are nearby.
211 East Flamingo Rd.
Tel: (702) 365 5000.
www.theplatinumhotel.com

Food and drink

A 24-hour city attracting millions of visitors from all corners of the globe needs to offer an extensive selection of restaurants and cuisine. Whether you want fine dining, American home cooking, Japanese, Mexican, Moroccan or Italian, there are hundreds of establishments to choose from in Las Vegas. Pick up a local What's On *guide or similar publication as soon as you arrive to find offers and information on the city's best eating spots.*

Restaurants

Price guide per person, for a main course:

★	Under $10
★★	$10–20
★★★	$21–30
★★★★	Over $30

In-N-Out Burger ★

Praised for serving the best burger in the city – indeed the world, according to its legions of fans – In-N-Out is fast, fresh and the biggest bang for your buck in Vegas. Don't pass up the hand-cut fries and thick shakes.
2900 West Sahara Ave.
Tel: (800) 786 1000. Open: Sun–Thur 10.30am–1.00am, Fri & Sat 10.30am–1.30am.

Triple 7 Restaurant & Microbrewery ★

This no-frills microbrewery is the best bet for standard American pub fare, with a raucous sports bar backdrop in the Downtown area. For midriff havoc, try the piquant chicken wings.
Main Street Station Hotel, 200 North Main St. Tel: (702) 387 1896.
Open: daily 11am–7am.

Firefly ★★

This East Side tapas joint has a vibrant neighbourhood atmosphere and delicious small plates that push the boundaries of traditional Spanish tapas; the tuna tartare, stuffed dates, filet mignon sliders and Manchego Mac 'n' Cheese are all highly recommended. Fuel your appetite with the full-bodied pitchers of Sangria.
3900 Paradise Rd. Tel: (702) 369 3971.
Open: daily 11.30am–2am.

Gandhi India's Cuisine ★★

Voted best Indian restaurant in Las Vegas and offering tandoori dishes, seafood, meat curries and vegetarian meals, this restaurant also offers an all-you-can-eat lunch buffet.
4080 Paradise Rd. Tel: (702) 734 0094.
Open: daily, lunch 11am–2.30pm, dinner 5–10.30pm.

Grotto ★★

Classic Italian fare at the Golden
Nugget in Grotto, where they have their
own pizza oven and home-made pasta,
as well as recommendations from the
Michelin Guide.
The Golden Nugget Hotel,
129 Fremont St. Tel: (702) 385 7111.
Open: Sun–Thur 11.30am–10.30pm,
Fri & Sat 11.30am–11.30pm.

Harley-Davidson Café ★★

Featuring the largest display of
Harley-Davidson memorabilia and
American dishes that include pasta,
chicken, barbecue, salads and
sandwiches. There is also a Harley-
Davidson shop in the restaurant.
3725 Las Vegas Blvd S.
Tel: (702) 740 4555.
Open: Sun–Thur 11am–midnight,
Fri & Sat 11am–2am.

Mon Ami Gabi ★★

Watch the world rush by on the Strip,
or enjoy the Fountains at Bellagio
while you dine alfresco outside Paris.
Wonderful wines complement French
cuisine that includes cassoulet,
shallot steak and bouillabaisse, all
created by award-winning chef
Gabino Sotelino.
Paris Las Vegas, 3645 Las Vegas Blvd S.
Tel: (702) 944 4224.
Open: breakfast daily 7–11am,
brunch Sat & Sun 11am–3pm, lunch
Mon–Fri 11.30am–3.45pm, dinner
Sun–Thur 4–11pm, Fri & Sat
4pm–midnight.

Nine Fine Irishmen ★★

This popular bar has a hearty menu
that is hard to resist. Choose from main
courses such as beer-battered fish and
chips or shepherd's pie infused with
port, then follow up with Bushmills
bread pudding with whiskey cream.
New York-New York Hotel and Casino,
3790 Las Vegas Blvd S. Tel: (702) 740
6969. Open: daily 11am–11pm.

The Pub ★★

This microbrewery offers home-made
beers, live music and an extensive food
menu that includes pizzas, gourmet
wraps and sandwiches.
Monte Carlo Resort & Casino,
3770 Las Vegas Blvd S.
Tel: (702) 730 7777. Open: Sun–Thur
11am–11pm, Fri & Sat 11am–3am

Harley-Davidsons parked outside the Harley-
Davidson Café

Rainforest Café ★★

With animated elephants and gorillas, waterfalls and a saltwater aquarium, this lively restaurant is popular with all the family and offers American cuisine and the chain's signature dishes.
MGM Grand Hotel & Casino, 3799 Las Vegas Blvd S. Tel: (702) 891 8580. Open: daily 8am–11pm, Fri & Sat until midnight.

Bartolotta Ristorante di Mare ★★★

Paul Bartolotta's Italian seafood mecca serves the finest Mediterranean fish in the city. You can dine inside, in the charming rustic dining room, or alfresco, overlooking the Wynn's serene lake. It's expensive but unforgettable.
Wynn, 3131 Las Vegas Blvd S. Tel: (702) 770 9966. Open: nightly dinner 5.30–10pm.

Bradley Ogden ★★★

The eponymous chef works his magic before your eyes in this elegant Caesars restaurant, which serves New American dishes with a twist. The sophisticated but laid-back ambience makes for relaxing event dining.
Caesars Palace, 3570 Las Vegas Blvd S. Tel: (702) 731 7731. Open: Wed–Sun 5–11pm.

Japonais ★★★

One of the latest offerings at the Mirage, this chichi Japanese fusion restaurant serves innovative dishes, such as chestnut-encrusted chicken with shitake rice stuffing, in a stylish Zen setting.
Mirage, 3400 Las Vegas Blvd S. Tel: (702) 792 7800. Open: dinner Sun, Mon, Thur 5–10pm, Fri & Sat 5–11pm; lounge & bar Mon–Wed noon–1am, Thur & Fri noon–2am.

Rosemary's ★★★

Reservations must be made weeks in advance for this epicurean feast served in a charming dining room by superlative waiting staff. Expect a wide range of unique and tantalising flavours: bass with 'hushpuppies' in a creole meuniere sauce and twice-baked Parmesan soufflé.
West Sahara Promenade, 8125 West Sahara Ave. Tel: (702) 869 2251. Open: lunch Fri 11.30am–2pm; nightly dinner 5.30pm–close.

Eiffel Tower Restaurant ★★★★

Enjoy cocktails or caviar and wonderful French cuisine created by award-winning chef J Joho. The dining room provides fantastic views of the Strip, 11 storeys below.
Paris Las Vegas, 3645 Las Vegas Blvd S. Tel: (702) 948 6937. Open: daily lunch 11.30am–2.30pm; dinner Sun–Thur 5–10.15pm, Fri & Sat until 10.45pm.

Hyakumi Japanese Restaurant & Sushi Bar ★★★★

Translated as '100 tastes', Hyakumi offers 40 varieties of sushi and sashimi, along with many other Japanese dishes from the menu. Sit at the sushi bar or have your food prepared at a tableside grill. Highly recommended.

Caesars Palace, 3570 Las Vegas Blvd S. Tel: (702) 731 7731. Open: daily, lunch 11am–3.30pm, dinner 5–11pm.

N9NE ★★★★

Winner of the Best in Vegas for 2005, this highly acclaimed steakhouse also features a champagne and caviar bar within an elegant setting, with leather, suede and bright metallic furnishings. *Palms Casino Resort, 4321 West Flamingo Ave. Tel: (702) 942 7777. Open: Sun–Thur 5.30–10pm, Fri & Sat until 11pm.*

Top of the World ★★★★

Dress up for the evening and enjoy a meal in one of Las Vegas's top gourmet restaurants. This impressive restaurant offers 360-degree views of the city from the top of the Stratosphere Tower as it slowly rotates over a period of one hour.
The Stratosphere Tower Hotel & Casino, 2000 Las Vegas Blvd S. Tel: (702) 380 7711. Open: 11am–2.30pm & 5.30–10.15pm, Fri & Sat until 10.45pm.

The Top of the World restaurant towers high above Vegas

The Las Vegas buffet

With dishes from around the world, Las Vegas is famed for its all-you-can-eat buffets. Be prepared to put on a little weight after returning to fill your plate time after time, as there is so much to choose from. Most restaurants offer breakfast, lunch and evening buffets.

Price guide per person, for dinner (excluding tax and gratuities):

★	Under $15
★★	$15–$20
★★★	Over $20

Most hotels offer a buffet and serve breakfast from 7am, lunch from 11.30am and dinner from the late afternoon, usually between 4pm and 5pm.

Circus Buffet ★

One of the largest in Las Vegas, this buffet is also one of the most reasonable; the breakfast here is particularly popular.
Circus Circus, 2880 Las Vegas Blvd S.
Tel: (702) 734 0410.

Lotus of Siam ★

What it lacks in décor and location, this oriental hidden treasure makes up for with its superlative Asian cuisine that specialises in northern Thai dishes for its buffet lunch. Locals consistently rate Lotus one of the top and most inexpensive restaurants in town.
953 East Sahara Ave.
Tel: (702) 735 3033.

The Buffet at the Golden Nugget ★★

Known for its Sunday champagne brunch and carved meats, the Golden Nugget is a popular buffet located in the centre of Downtown Las Vegas.
Golden Nugget Hotel,
129 East Fremont St.
Tel: (702) 385 7111.

The Buffet – Las Vegas Hilton ★★

Just off the Strip, this buffet offers fresh fruit, salads and delicious main courses, including a carving station, as well as desserts prepared by world-renowned pastry chef Stanton Ho. Champagne brunches are also available.
Las Vegas Hilton, 3000 Paradise Rd.
Tel: (702) 732 5111.

Feast Buffet ★★

Dinner includes prime rib and seafood and many food stations offering a huge variety of dishes. This resort is featured on the US television reality show *American Casino*. Highly recommended.
Green Valley Ranch Resort & Spa, 2300 Paseo Verde Pkwy, Henderson.
Tel: (702) 617 7777.

MGM Grand Buffet ★★

This is all you can eat Hollywood-style, with carving stations, seafood, a bountiful salad bar and mouthwatering desserts. The MGM Grand also offers a weekend champagne brunch.
MGM Grand Hotel & Casino,
3799 Las Vegas Blvd S.
Tel: (702) 891 1111.

Bellagio Buffet ★★★

The all-you-can-eat concept reaches its zenith with sushi stations, kobe beef and exotic fruits galore in this homage to global cuisine and insatiable gourmands.
Bellagio, 3600 Las Vegas Blvd S.
Tel: (702) 693 8255.

Carnival World Buffet ★★★

Voted the best buffet in Las Vegas, with more than 300 freshly prepared dishes, including Italian, Asian, barbecue and sushi, and live cooking stations. There are also over 70 varieties of home-made pies, cakes and pastries.
Rio All-Suite Hotel & Casino,
3700 West Flamingo Rd.
Tel: (702) 777 7777.

Cravings ★★★

Wander through streets lined with restaurants within a beautiful village setting, with 11 cooking stations and live cooking broadcasts and cuisine from around the world.
Mirage, 3400 Las Vegas Blvd S.
Tel: (702) 791 7111.

Sterling Brunch ★★★

Bally's Sunday-only extravaganza features lobster, filet mignon and caviar washed down with Perrier Jovët. Extremely popular. Patience, good credit and expandable clothing are required. Reservations advised.
Bally's Las Vegas, 3654 Las Vegas Blvd. S. Tel: (702) 739 4111.

Le Village Buffet ★★★

This highly acclaimed buffet includes sweet and savoury crêpes, delicious main courses, seafood, cheeses and freshly baked French breads all in a beautiful village setting.
Paris Las Vegas, 3655 Las Vegas Blvd S.
Tel: (877) 796 2096.

There are dishes on offer from around the world at Cravings

Dining in Las Vegas

Along with the luxurious hotel resorts and entertainment, dining is unsurpassed in Las Vegas. When you arrive at McCarran Airport, mouth-watering advertisements boast world-famous chefs and all-you-can-eat buffets in a city that offers 24-hour dining, themed restaurants and gourmet cuisine from every corner of the globe. You don't have to stay on the Strip to indulge in world-class cuisine. As Las Vegas builds its community credentials, more and more neighbourhood joints are opening, serving fine food at more affordable prices and in more intimate settings.

All you can eat

Eighty per cent of Las Vegas visitors will opt for the all-you-can-eat buffet. Offered in almost every resort, diners can choose from seafood, carved meats and international cuisine. The first Las Vegas Buffet was the Midnight Chuck Wagon in the El Rancho during the 1940s.

Themed restaurants

All the main themed eating establishments have some of their flagship restaurants in Las Vegas.

Look out for the Planet Hollywood Resort, the Hard Rock Cafe, the Harley-Davidson Café and the Rainforest Café in the MGM Grand, complete with its waterfalls and aquarium, while motorsports fanatics can enjoy the NASCAR Café at the Sahara.

Seafood

Enjoy the culinary creations of chef Emeril Lagasse in Emeril's at the MGM Grand and Tom Moloney's AquaKnox at The Venetian. Seafood is on many buffet menus, particularly at the Paradise Garden Buffet at the Flamingo and the Market Square Buffet at Harrah's. Las Vegas also offers countless oyster bars, lobster houses and sushi bars, such as the Hyakumi Japanese Restaurant & Sushi Bar at Caesars Palace or Nobu at the Hard Rock Hotel.

All American

Las Vegas is famed for its steak houses and prime-rib specials. Enjoy the glamour and old-school ambience of Steakhouse at the Circus Circus hotel, or try the celebrated Charlie Palmer Steak at the Four Seasons. The major US steakhouse chains are also represented: Ruth's Chris, Joe's and Del Frisco's.

Wolfgang Puck Bar & Grill at the MGM Grand.

Fine dining

While Picasso and Le Cirque at Bellagio have both earned Mobil five-star ratings, Las Vegas offers countless gourmet restaurants to satisfy the most discerning palate. Top names, including André Rochat, Jean-Marie Josselin and Sirio Maccioni, are among the many world-famous chefs who offer their gourmet delights in Las Vegas. The celebrated chef and restauranteur Wolfgang Puck also has establishments here, such as the

Loosen that belt...

Your choice is endless. You can eat breakfast 24 hours a day, or choose from a world of cuisines that include American, Asian, Brazilian, Chinese, Cuban, French, Indian, Indonesian, Irish, Italian, Japanese, Mexican, Moroccan, Persian and Vietnamese. And to wash it all down, Las Vegas is home to many of the US master sommeliers and establishments that have earned critical acclaim for their wine lists.

The shop at the Rainforest Café is appropriately fitted out

Entertainment

Never were you offered so much choice for entertainment. On stage, with production shows, comedy clubs, world-class celebrities and magicians, Las Vegas has it all. From the early lounge shows featuring legends like Louis Prima and Nat King Cole, the city has always presented high-profile celebrities, now adding Tom Jones, the Rolling Stones, Tony Bennett, Dwight Yoakam, Paul McCartney, Neil Diamond, Céline Dion and Elton John to its unrivalled listings.

While you are in Las Vegas, do not miss acclaimed production shows such as *Mystère*, *KÀ*, '*O*' and *Zumanity* by Cirque du Soleil or Dragone's *Le Rêve* at Wynn. *Phantom of the Opera* is showing at The Venetian, and Monty Python's *Spamalot* was a recent production at Wynn. Interact with the players in dinner shows such as *Tournament of the Kings*, or *Tony n' Tina's Wedding* where you can be a guest at the chaotic reception, complete with a drunken minister and pregnant bridesmaid. There are variety shows with a difference, such as a glitzy *Jubilee!* at Bally's, which includes the sinking of the *Titanic* every night, or *V – the Ultimate Variety Show* at the Planet Hollywood Hotel, which features some of the most unusual acts in the business.

Most production shows offer their own blend of comedy and entertainment, but the city is also home to several comedy clubs, such as Improv at Harrah's, Riviera Comedy Club or The Comedy Stop at the Tropicana, which features three up-and-coming comedians on a bill that changes weekly. Rita Rudner is in residence at Harrah's, where she was voted Comedian of the Year, while the wacky Carrot Top is a frequent visitor to the Strip, along with award-winning headliners such as Ray Romano, Jackie Mason and Jerry Seinfeld, who often performs at Caesars Palace. The Rio offers family shows with Penn & Teller, combining magic and comedy, and the Flamingo presents Nathan Burton (*www.nathanburton.com*), another witty magician who performs a regular afternoon show.

Known as Sin City, Las Vegas is also renowned for adult shows such as *Crazy Horse Paris*, *Bite* or *Fantasy*. You can see uncensored hypnotists such as Anthony Cools at Paris, who claims that you should leave all inhibitions at home, and has audiences returning night after night in case they miss out on more outrageous antics.

In a city filled with tribute acts you can see shows dedicated to Elvis Presley and the Beatles, or sip cocktails with the Rat Pack at the Plaza in *The Rat Pack is Back*. Only in Las Vegas could you see Elvis Presley sharing a stage with Britney Spears and Christina Aguilera in *American Superstars* at the Stratosphere, while *Barbara and*

Frank: The Concert That Never Was, at the Riviera, introduces Streisand and Sinatra tribute artists interspersed with video montages of the Vegas legends.

In short, there are more shows and opportunities for entertainment than you could fit into a single visit to Las Vegas. *See the guide to must-see productions on pp150–56, and suggestions for free entertainment on p157.*

Advertising *Jubilee!* at Bally's on the Strip

The Rat Pack

In January 1960 the Rat Pack held court at the Sands Hotel. Frank Sinatra, Dean Martin, Sammy Davis Jr, Peter Lawford and Joey Bishop were in Las Vegas to film the classic casino heist *Ocean's Eleven* and every evening, after production wrapped, they took to the stage at the Copa Room.

Hotel rooms were booked throughout the city, as people clambered for the chance to see Frank and his buddies on stage. On some nights, only one or two would appear, but on lucky occasions, audiences were entertained by the whole pack.

The Venetian was built on the site of the Sands Hotel

They were the ultimate Kings of Cool, and breezed through filming, refusing to commit more than a single take, as they ad-libbed through each scene with drinks in hand. The same happened on stage. Dean Martin would drift into the spotlight 'direct from the bar', as he was introduced, and with drink in one hand, cigarette in the other, he would croon effortlessly through *Volare* or *That's Amore*. Dean had been performing in Las Vegas since he first partnered Jerry Lewis in the 1940s, and was followed on stage at the Sands by another Vegas regular, Sammy Davis Jr, who first played the city when he was 19. As a performer, Sammy burst with energy, and his powerhouse vocals and frantic tap routines were exhausting just to witness, while Frank, Dean and the rest of the pack pulled up a bar stool on stage and watched him. As for the chairman of the board, Frank Sinatra was also a huge name in Las Vegas. He made his first appearance

Sammy Davis Jr

at the Desert Inn in 1941 and remained a headliner in the city for over 40 years. 'This is Frank's world,' Dean would quip. 'We just live in it.'

The Rat Pack Summit was named in jest after the Paris Summit, which gathered Dwight D Eisenhower, the then US president, with French and Soviet leaders. Frank had his own political aspirations, and publicly backed John F Kennedy's campaign for the White House, inviting Kennedy's brother-in-law Peter Lawford into his fold. Writer-comedian Joey Bishop led the humour for the pack, but collectively their antics brought the house to hysterics. As a mini-bar was wheeled on stage, they sipped Martinis and entertained their celebrity-filled audiences until the early hours, making a permanent mark on entertainment history.

Backstage, the party was just beginning.

RAT PACK TRIBUTE SHOWS

Share a toast with Frank and his buddies in one of the Rat Pack tribute shows in Las Vegas. These highly acclaimed productions, complete with swingin' big bands, have taken residence at various Vegas nightspots over the years, with recent shows taking place at the Plaza. Check the printed show guides or your hotel box office to find the latest venue.

SHOWTIME ON THE STRIP

Las Vegas offers the very best in entertainment and the demand for many of its world-class production shows means that you may have to book tickets as soon as you have confirmed your travel arrangements. However, while you are in Vegas, the choice is still endless and many shows offer discounts or special deals, which you can find in the local guides located in most hotels.

Starting prices for shows, per adult:

★   Under $25
★★ $25–$50
★★★ $51–$100
★★★★   Over $100

Production shows

Blue Man Group ★★

The stars of this show are three bright blue bald men who have won over audiences all over the globe. If your curiosity wins out, you will be rewarded by an outrageous performance, but beware: you will be given a protective poncho if you sit too near the front!
Venetian Resort Hotel & Casino, 3355 Las Vegas Blvd S. Shows: daily 7pm & 10pm.

LOVE ★★★

One of the most impressive and talked-about Cirque du Soleil shows to hit Vegas in a long time has been this tribute to the Beatles, *LOVE*. It uses the band's original music, specially created in their own Abbey Road Studios in London by their recording manager, Sir George Martin, and his son Giles. A cast of 60 interpret the music and lyrics, and the songs are played through 6,500 speakers, making the show as impressive to hear as to see. Visually, the show is much more than the usual special effects, as the cast bring some of the song's characters to life and turn the show into a kind of musical biography going back to the start of the Beatles in Liverpool. It's the kind of show that people can, and do, see more than once.
Mirage. 3400 Las Vegas Blvd S. Tel: (702) 791 7111. Shows: Thur–Mon 7pm & 9.30pm.

Jubilee! ★★★

With million-dollar sets and costumes by Emmy Award-winning designer Bob Mackie, *Jubilee!* is voted as the best showgirl revue in Las Vegas. This must-see spectacular includes singers, dancer acrobats and a dramatic scene featuring the sinking of the *Titanic*.
Bally's Las Vegas, 3645 Las Vegas Blvd S. Tel: (702) 739 4111. Shows: daily 7.30pm & 10.30pm. No show Fri. All-access backstage tickets can also be purchased.

KÀ ★★★★

Described as Cirque du Soleil's most ambitious production, *KÀ* presents the tale of two Imperial twins and their epic journey through life. A cast of more than 80 performers combine martial arts, acrobatics, puppetry,

interactive video projections and pyrotechnics to create an exciting and awe-inspiring performance.
MGM Grand Hotel & Casino, 3799 Las Vegas Blvd S. Tel: (702) 891 1111. Shows: 7pm & 9.30pm Tue–Sat.

Lance Burton, Master Magician ★★★
This acclaimed illusionist is a Las Vegas favourite. In this family show, Burton makes a whole convertible disappear and often enlists the audience to help on stage.

Le Rêve is based at the Wynn

The Liberace Museum is the venue for the *Liberace and Me* show

The Monte Carlo Resort & Casino, 3770 Las Vegas Blvd S. Tel: (702) 730 7777. Shows: Tue–Sat 7pm.

Legends in Concert ★

The original Las Vegas tribute show, running for over 20 years with an

ever-changing list of stars that includes Elvis, Ricky Martin, Prince and Madonna. Check local guides for more discounts and promotions for this popular show.
Harrah's Las Vegas, 3475 Las Vegas Blvd S. Tel: (702) 369 5111. Shows: Tue, Thur & Sun 6.30pm, 7.30pm and 10pm.

Le Rêve: A Small Collection of Imperfect Dreams ★★★
With every seat at centre stage, *Le Rêve* features a cast of artists and athletes from around the world, performing outstanding acrobatic feats. Characters rise, fall and are created from fire, rain and the infinite depths of *Le Rêve's* aquatic stage.
Wynn Las Vegas, 3131 Las Vegas Blvd S. Tel: (702) 770 7000. Shows: Fri–Tue 7pm & 9.30pm.

The Lion King ★★★
Disney's *The Lion King*, the hit musical based on the original 1994 film, has been seen by over 50 million people worldwide, and the Vegas production has been just as acclaimed. It mixes a live cast with puppet animals in a family-friendly story but with some nicely scary moments.
Mandalay Bay, 3950 Las Vegas Blvd S. Tel: (702) 632 7777. Shows: Mon–Thur 7.30pm, Sat & Sun 4pm and 8pm. No show Fri.

Menopause The Musical ★★
This spoof on the ageing process is a riotous performance of hot flushes and screaming rages with broader appeal than you would imagine.
Luxor, 3900 Las Vegas Blvd. Tel: (702) 262 4400. Shows: Wed–Mon 5.30pm, Tue 5pm & 8.30pm.

Liberace and Me ★
This short but great-value show could not be better placed than amid the pomp and splendour of the Liberace Museum. Playing Liberace's legendary rhinestone piano, Wes Winters invites full audience participation in celebrating the sparkling career of Mr Showmanship.
Liberace Museum, 1775 East Tropicana Ave. Tel: (702) 798 5595. Shows: Tue, Wed & Sat 1pm.

Mystère by Cirque du Soleil ★★★
Playing in Las Vegas for over ten years, *Mystère* unravels the human potential with a cast of over 72 gymnasts, acrobats, clowns, dancers, singers and musicians.
TI, 3300 Las Vegas Blvd S. Tel: (702) 796 9999. Shows: Sat–Wed 7pm & 9.30pm.

O by Cirque du Soleil ★★★
With 81 artists performing in, around, over and under a pool of water 7.5m (25ft) deep, 'O' is a breathtaking presentation of theatre through the ages.
Bellagio, 3600 Las Vegas Blvd S. Tel: (702) 693 7111. Shows: Wed–Sun 7.30pm & 10pm.

Penn & Teller ★★★

With the tagline 'If you're lucky, nobody gets injured', the bad boys of magic have earned critical acclaim across the globe for bringing a new dynamic to this old craft.
Rio All-Suite Hotel & Casino, 3700 West Flamingo Rd. Tel: (702) 777 7777. Shows: Sat–Wed 9pm.

The Rat Pack is Back ★★★

There have been several Rat Pack tribute shows in Las Vegas, including this show at the Greek Isles, where Frank Sinatra, Dean Martin, Sammy Davis Jr and comedian Joey Bishop take you back to their swinging era of Las Vegas in the 1960s. A hilarious show with a live big band.
Plaza, 1 Main St. Tel: (702) 386 2444. Shows: daily 6pm (with dinner) or 7.30pm.

Tony n' Tina's Wedding ★★★

With a ticket price that includes dinner, tips and a champagne toast, join Tony and Tina as a guest at their tacky wedding reception, and look on while the other guests and the family cause havoc. You can even pose for the wedding photographer in a show that brings audience participation to a whole new level.
Rio All-Suite Hotel & Casino, 3700 West Flamingo Rd. Tel: (702) 777 7777. Shows: Mon–Sat 7pm. VIP tickets are also available.

Tournament of Kings ★★

Forget the cutlery and your table manners in this riotous medieval joust. With over 100 performers, this is a popular show for all the family.
Excalibur Hotel & Casino, 3850 Las Vegas Blvd S. Tel: (702) 597 7777. Shows: Mon–Thur 6pm, Fri–Sun 6pm & 8.30pm.

Hypnosis Unleashed ★★

An adults-only show with hypnotists Terry Stokes and Michael Johns, who push the boundaries of what they can persuade people to do by their powers of suggestion.
Tropicana, 3801 Las Vegas Blvd S. Tel: (800) 829 9034. Shows: daily 9pm.

Headliners

There are always headliners on the Strip. Some are in residence, and stars such as Tony Bennett, Jerry Seinfeld, Neil Diamond and Tom Jones have recently appeared along with the many entertainers who include the city on their tours. At the time of writing, ongoing headliners included the following:

Elton John: The Red Piano ★★★★

Winning several awards since opening in 2004, this show features Elton John and his vivid red piano set before the Colosseum's huge LED screen, which projects rich, and sometimes provocative, imagery of Hollywood and Las Vegas icons,

to accompany hits ranging from *Rocket Man* to *Candle In The Wind*.
Caesars Palace, 3570 Las Vegas Blvd S.
Tel: (702) 731 7110.
Shows: daily 8pm.

Barry Manilow in Manilow: Music and Passion ★★★

After a successful run at the Hilton, pop legend Manilow has moved to the Paris for an all-new show featuring classic pop songs from *Copacabana* to *Bermuda Triangle*, as well as famed ballads such as *I Write The Songs*. One not to miss.
Paris Las Vegas, 3655 Las Vegas Blvd.
Tel: (800) 745 3000.
Shows: Thur–Sun 7.30pm.

Cher ★★★★

Taking over from Bette Midler at the stunning 4,000-seat Colosseum at Caesars Palace, Cher performs her hits and showcases her stunning costumes too.
Caesars Palace, 3570 Las Vegas Blvd S.
Tel: (702) 731 7110. Shows: Tue & Wed, Sat & Sun 7.30pm.

Entertainment venues

For your one chance to see your favourite entertainers on tour, make sure you check listings for venues such as the MGM Grand Garden Arena, which has hosted the Eagles, Sting, Jimmy Buffett, Paul McCartney and the Billboard Music Awards. The

Catch a show at the Tropicana or the MGM Grand

House of Blues at Mandalay Bay always has a packed entertainment schedule and has featured Willie Nelson, CMT's Most Wanted Live Tour and Lisa Marie Presley, while the Joint at the Hard Rock Hotel has showcased acts such as David Bowie, KD Lang and Santana.

The *Show in the Sky* at the Rio

Free entertainment

Just walking along the Strip, visiting the luxury resorts or people-watching in the casinos can provide hours of free entertainment, in addition to a multitude of free museums, wildlife attractions, stage shows and neon spectaculars, which are too numerous to list here in full.

Mermaid Swims

This choreographed underwater show features mermaids and mermen among over 4,000 tropical fish in the Silverton's 443,000-litre (117,000-gallon) aquarium.
Silverton Hotel and Casino,
3333 Blue Diamond Rd.
Tel: (702) 363 7777.
Shows: Thur 2.15–8.45pm, Fri & Sat
2.15–9.45pm, Sun 11.30am–6.45pm.

Bonnie & Clyde Exhibit

See the original newspaper reports on the couple, an intricate necklace made by Clyde while in prison, and their famous getaway car.
Primm Valley Resort, 31900 Las Vegas
Blvd S, Interstate 15 south on the
California border. Tel: (702) 386 7867.
Open: 24 hours.

CBS Television City Research Center

Register for free tickets then watch the latest new television pilots where you can offer your own opinion on their future in television.
Located at the MGM Grand, 3799 Las
Vegas Blvd S. Tel: (702) 891 5776. Open:
daily 10am–8.30pm.

FREE ATTRACTIONS YOU MUST NOT MISS IN LAS VEGAS

The *Fremont Street Experience* (*see pp74–6*)
The Fountains at Bellagio (*see p38*)
MGM Grand Lion Habitat (*see p57*)
The Mirage Volcano (*see p49*)
The Neon Museum (*see p78*)
The *Sirens of TI* (*see p91*)
The Talking Statues at Caesars (*see p41*)

Show in the Sky

Floats are suspended above the crowd as the Rio presents its own Mardi Gras Carnival in the Masquerade Village.
Rio All-Suite Hotel & Casino,
3700 West Flamingo Rd.
Tel: (702) 777 7777.
Shows: Thur–Sun hourly 7pm–midnight.

Penske–Wynn Ferrari–Maserati

Some of the rarest and most expensive luxury cars are on display in this 9,300sq m (100,000sq ft) showroom. Many price tags are in excess of $700,000, including Steve Wynn's $1.4-million Enzo Ferrari.
Wynn Las Vegas, 3131 Las Vegas Blvd S.
Tel: (702) 770 2000. Open: Mon–Sat
9am–6pm.

The World's Largest Permanent Circus

Live circus acts every 30 minutes, from trapeze artists and acrobats to tightrope walkers.
Circus Circus Hotel & Casino,
2880 Las Vegas Blvd S.
Tel: (702) 734 0410.
Shows: daily 11am–midnight.

Shopping

Leave plenty of room in your suitcase when you pack for Las Vegas. Within an 8km (5-mile) radius of the Strip there are over 2.3 million sq m (25 million sq ft) of retail outlets, from hotel shops and designer malls to entire outlet villages.

The main resorts all have shopping areas, such as Bally's Avenue Shoppes, Le Boulevard at Paris, Mandalay Bay Shops and Mandalay Place, Masquerade Village at the Rio, MGM Grand Star Lane Shops, Monte Carlo Street of Dreams, New York-New York Shops, Street of Shops at the Mirage or the Tower Shops at Stratosphere. Some of the larger shopping malls offer restaurants, entertainment and free attractions.

Away from the Strip, there are many even larger shopping malls and outlet centres, ideal places to buy designer goods at bargain prices.
Shopping centres on the Strip are usually open from around 10am until 10pm.

The Las Vegas Strip
The Forum Shops at Caesars
Known for its talking statues and beautiful interior landscaping, after a recent extension the Forum Shops feature over 63,000sq m (700,000sq ft) of retail stores that include Louis Vuitton, Escada, Gucci, Guess,

Christian Dior, NIKETOWN, and BOSS HUGO BOSS, as well as several restaurants, including Wolfgang Puck's famed Spago and Planet Hollywood. Caesars is also home to the Appian Way, with 14 upmarket retailers, marble walkways, statues of Joe Louis and Michelangelo's David, along with a Brahma shrine and the Palace temple. Shops include Cartier, Le Paradis, Galerie Michelangelo, Ancient Creations, Art in Crystal and Gevril. (*See also pp40–41.*)
Caesars Palace, 3570 Las Vegas Blvd S.
www.caesarspalace.com

The Fashion Show Mall
This multi-level mall in the centre of the Strip offers nearly 180,000sq m (2 million sq ft) of retail stores that include Neiman-Marcus, Saks Fifth Avenue, Bloomingdale's Home, Macy's, Dillard's, Diesel and Nordstrom. An impressive new food hall has recently been added to the shopping centre, with a balcony overlooking the Strip.

Enjoy the stately interior at the Forum Shops

wine merchants Le Cave, or find children's toys at Les Enfants, along with La Vogue boutique and the Presse Parisian-style newsstand.
Paris Las Vegas, 3655 Las Vegas Blvd S. Located where Paris joins Bally's. www.parislasvegas.com

Via Bellagio
Within Bellagio's luxurious surroundings, this shopping promenade offers over 9,290sq m (100,000sq ft) of designer boutiques that include Chanel, Giorgio Armani, Prada, Tiffany & Co, Yves Saint Laurent, Fendi and Gucci.
Bellagio, 3600 Las Vegas Blvd S. www.bellagio.com

Off-Strip shopping
The Boulevard Mall
With 100,000sq m (1.13 million sq ft) of retail outlets, this is one of Nevada's largest shopping centres, with 140 shops that include Foot Locker, Old Navy, JC Penney, Sears and Macy's.
The Boulevard Mall, 3528 Maryland Parkway, Las Vegas. www.boulevardmall.com

Galleria at Sunset
This mall, 19km (12 miles) east of Las Vegas, in Henderson, includes JC Penney, Gap, Dillard's, Cache, Champs Sports, Victoria's Secret and The Body Shop, along with a 600-seat food court.
1300 West Sunset Rd, Henderson. www.galleriaatsunset.com

3200 Las Vegas Blvd S. www.thefashionshow.com

Grand Canal Shoppes at The Venetian
Surrounding the Grand Canal, with street entertainers and the beautiful St Mark's Square, this shopping centre has over 45,000sq m (500,000sq ft) of retail outlets that include Banana Republic, Bebe and Rockport. Like Caesars and Bellagio, this is a great resort for fashion shoppers. (*See also pp42 & 51.*)
Venetian Resort Hotel & Casino, 3355 Las Vegas Blvd S. www.thegrandcanalshoppes.com

Le Boulevard at Paris Las Vegas
Shop through Parisian streets featuring authentic French boutiques such as the

The Fashion Show Mall on the Las Vegas Strip

The Meadows Mall

With two levels of shops and five courtyards, the Meadows Mall includes Dillard's, Macy's, JC Penney and Sears. The mall is located on US 95 Expressway, although it provides a trolley service from the Downtown Transportation Center.

4300 Meadows Lane, Las Vegas.
www.meadowsmall.com

Outlet shopping

Fashion Outlet Las Vegas

Located 56km (35 miles) south of the city in Primm, on the Nevada–California border, this outlet offers over 100 brand-name shops, including Tommy Hilfiger, Polo Ralph Lauren, Kenneth Cole, Bath & Body Works and Wilson's Leather. There are shuttles from the Las Vegas Strip from New York-New York and the MGM Grand.

32100 Las Vegas Blvd S, Primm.
www.fashionoutletlasvegas.com

Las Vegas Outlet Center

Frequent visitors will remember this as Belz Factory Outlet, just south of the Las Vegas Strip. With countless brand-

ONLY IN LAS VEGAS ...

... can you find the **Bonanza Gift Shop**, located next to the Stratosphere, where you can buy every Vegas souvenir possible from personalised dice to mini slot machines. Gambling fanatics can purchase gaming memorabilia at the **Gamblers General Store**, Downtown on 800 South Main Street, or the **Casino Legends Hall of Fame** gift shop in the Tropicana. You can find the very best vintage clothing and all things retro at **The Attic**, located at 1018 South Main Street.

name bargains at 20–70 per cent discount, shops include Reebok, Levi's, Liz Claiborne New York and Nike. You can get a Citizens Area Transit (CAT) bus from the Las Vegas Strip to the centre, or it is a very short drive by taxi or car.
7400 Las Vegas Blvd S.
www.premiumoutlets.com

Las Vegas Premium Outlets

Over 40,000sq m (435,000sq ft) of stores in a new $80 million shopping centre that includes over 100 designer names such as Armani Exchange, Dolce & Gabbana, Guess, Kenneth Cole, Lacoste, Polo Ralph Lauren Factory Store, St John, Ted Baker, Theory and the Tommy Hilfiger Company Store. Discounts range from 25 to 75 per cent.
875 South Grand Central Pkwy,
Las Vegas. www.premiumoutlets.com

The colourful exterior of Fashion Outlet Las Vegas

Sport and leisure

There are a multitude of sports and recreational facilities in Las Vegas and the surrounding areas, such as Red Rock Canyon, the Grand Canyon and Mount Charleston, which all offer outdoor activities from biking, climbing and watersports to backcountry adventures. Las Vegas is also famed for its championship golf courses and leading sports events, from boxing and basketball to rodeo challenges, while racing enthusiasts will find many events and activities at the Las Vegas Motor Speedway.

Escape from the neon and enjoy the breathtaking countryside by taking part in the many outdoor activities that cater for all levels of fitness.

Aerial activities

Take a relaxing balloon tour (*see p166*) or visit one of the many parachute and skydiving centres around Las Vegas. Beginners can also try skydiving indoors.

For the ultimate extremes in height and speed, you should try skydiving. Racing towards the earth from a distance of thousands of metres would give you the optimum view of the Strip, Las Vegas, and even four American states. Skydive Las Vegas offers the highest skydive in Las Vegas – 5km (3 miles) – and operates outside Las Vegas in Boulder City. If this is not for you, try the sport of body flight at Vegas Indoor Skydiving (*see p102*) and simulate the freefall experienced in skydiving within a vertical column of air that reaches speeds of up to 192kph (120mph).

Fishing

Lake Mead provides hundreds of kilometres of fishing shores offering bass, catfish, sunfish and rainbow trout, among other species. For information on fishing licences, contact the Nevada Division of Wildlife: *www.nevadadivisionofwildlife.org*. See *pp158–61* for more details.

Hiking

Most ambitious hikers would head straight for the Grand Canyon, but closer to Vegas in the Mount Charleston Wilderness there are several advanced trails ranging from 13–26km (8–16 miles), reaching elevations of 2,348–3,633m (7,705–11,918ft). All levels including beginners can visit Red Rock Canyon, which offers 22 trails reaching heights of up to 2,130m (*c.* 7,000ft), along with the bright red sands of the Valley of Fire State Park, with its easier routes that take you past 3,000-year-old Native American petroglyphs.

Horse riding
Horse riders can visit the fiery Red Rock Canyon, or Mount Charleston and the Spring Mountains National Recreation Area. These trails are very difficult and overnight camping with horses is not allowed.

Mountain and road biking
Advanced mountain riders can enjoy the Bootleg Canyon Trails in the Boulder City area, a scenic route that includes the steep (22 per cent gradient) Elevator Shaft, the 22km (14-mile) Elvis Presta Trail network in Spring Mountains, and the gruelling 8km (5-mile) Hurl in Red Rock Canyon. Easier routes include the Old Spanish Trail in Red Rock Canyon and the River Mountains Loop Trail in Henderson. Cyclists can take it easy on the Red Rock Canyon Scenic Loop or the 80km (50-mile) Blue Diamond Loop in Spring Mountain Ranch State Park.

Rock climbing
Experienced climbers can enjoy over 1,200 named routes in Red Rock Canyon, along with Mount Charleston, which also offers ice climbing from 2,400m (8,000ft). There are several indoor climbing venues in Las Vegas as well as centres that offer tuition. *See p169 for more information.*

Skiing and snowboarding
With fresh snow on Mount Charleston and the Spring Mountains it's hard to

There are countless routes for keen cyclists

believe you are in the middle of the desert. Trails are suitable for downhill and cross-country skiers.

Watersports
Lake Mead, the Colorado River and Lake Mojave are all excellent areas for kayaking and canoeing, while the stretch of river between the Hoover Dam and Lake Mojave is perfect for white-water rafting. Scuba divers of all levels can dive in both Lake Mojave and Lake Mead, where divers can also explore a cement tank used for the construction of the Hoover Dam.

Golf courses
Southern Nevada is home to over 60 public or semi-private golf courses with unrivalled views, beautiful landscaping

and lush foliage. Over 600,000 rounds of golf are played in the Las Vegas area each year and the city has also hosted major golfing events, including the LPGA Seniors Tour, the PGA tour and the NCAA Championships. Tiger Woods achieved his first PGA victory in Las Vegas, which has also welcomed amateur golfers such as former US President Bill Clinton and basketball hero Michael Jordan.

Starting prices per round:

★   Under $50

★★ $50–$100

★★★ $100–$200

★★★★ Over $200

Prices increase at weekends and in peak season.

Angel Park Golf Course ★★

Designed by Arnold Palmer and featuring two championship courses, a floodlit driving range and the Cloud Nine lighted short course.
100 South Rampart. Tel: (866) 447 4653. www.angelpark.com

Badlands Golf Club ★

This dramatic course, which takes in the scenic washes and canyons of the desert, was named one of Nevada's Top Ten courses by *Golf Digest* magazine.
9119 Alta Drive. Tel: (702) 363 0754. www.badlandsgc.com

Bali Hai Golf Club ★★★

Designed by Lee Schmidt and Brian Curley, with swaying palm trees over luscious fairways and white granite, Bali Hai's clubhouse is located at the Mandalay Bay site.
5160 Las Vegas Blvd. Tel: (866) 447 4653. www.balihaigolfclub.com

Bear's Best ★★

With views of the Las Vegas skyline and the Red Rock Mountains, Jack Nicklaus designed Bear's Best after designing 100 other courses. Bear's Best features replicas of the 18 best holes created by Nicklaus.
11111 West Flamingo Ave. Tel: (866) 385 8500. www.bearsbest.com

Callaway Golf Center/ Giant Golf Academy ★

Home to the Divine Nine course with waterfalls and desert vegetation, which is lit by night, this centre also includes a driving range overlooking the Strip and the Danny Gans Junior Golf Academy, which offers free golf tuition for ages 11 to 16.
Corner of Las Vegas Blvd and Sunset Rd. Tel: (702) 896 4100. www.cgclv.com

Las Vegas Golf Club ★

One of the oldest courses in Las Vegas and host to the Las Vegas City Amateur, the record on this friendly par-72 course is Monte Money's 58.
4300 West Washington. Tel: (702) 646 3003. www.lasvegasgc.com

Painted Desert ★★

Past host of the Nevada Open, this course forsakes green landscaping for

natural desert vegetation, with cactus and mesquite, the first of its kind in Las Vegas.
5555 Painted Mirage Way. Tel: (800) 468 7918. www.painteddesertgc.com

Paiute Golf Resort ★★
There are three championship courses at the Paiute Golf Resort: Sun Mountain, Snow Mountain and Wolf. If you've only time to play one then it has to be Wolf, the longest course in Nevada at 6,950m (7,604 yd).
10325 Nu Wav Kaiv Blvd. Tel: (702) 658 1400. www.lvpaiutegolf.com

Tuscany Golf Club ★★
Golf Magazine voted this par-72 course a few minutes from the Strip the best bang for your buck in Las Vegas two years in a row, while *Nevada Magazine* described it as the best course in southern Nevada.

901 Olivia Pkwy, Henderson.
Tel: (702) 951 1500.
www.tuscanygolfclub.com

The Wynn Golf and Country Club ★★★★
This world-class golf course was designed by Tom Fazio and features a par-70 course where 11 out of the 18 holes have water features.
Wynn Las Vegas, 3131 Las Vegas Blvd S. Tel: (702) 770 7000.

Desert activities
Enjoy the great outdoors with extreme sports, recreational activities, tours and cruises in the desert area surrounding Las Vegas. Some of these companies may arrange transfers from Las Vegas. Check your hotel box office or local magazines for details on more tours and excursions.

Angel Park Golf Course

Adventure Balloons

Offering early-morning hot-air balloon rides from the Las Vegas Strip to the mountains, the flagship balloon Smile High can carry up to eight passengers.

PO Box 27466, Las Vegas 89126. Tel: (702) 247 6905. www.smilerides.com

Adventure Photo Tours

Trips include photo safari tours in the Mojave Desert, where you can see Aztec sandstone formations, ancient Indian petroglyphs and pictographs, arches, gold mines, ghost towns, wild animals and desert flora.

3111 South Valley View Blvd, X-106. Tel: (702) 889 8687. www.adventurephototours.com

All American Adventure Tours

Tours include the Grand Canyon, the Hoover Dam, Indian Country, Colorado rafting, Lake Mead cruises, off-road tours and horse riding.

Transfers from Las Vegas. Tel: (702) 876 4600. www.americanadventuretours.com

Live the cowboy life not far from Las Vegas

Angler's Edge Guide Service
Offering guided fishing trips on Lake Mojave and Lake Mead, both of which are stocked with a wide variety of game fish.
915 Highland Trails Ave, Henderson. Tel: (702) 285 2814. www.fishanglersedge.com

Cowboy Trail Rides
Offering horse rides such as the Sunset Ride and BBQ in Red Rock Canyon, where you can enjoy steaks cooked on the campfire as you overlook the city of Las Vegas.
Located close to Downtown Las Vegas with transfers from the Strip. Tel: (702) 387 2457. www.cowboytrailrides.com

Eagle Rider Motorcycle Rental
Rent a shiny new Harley-Davidson and cruise across Nevada on models such as the Road King, Electra Glide, or the Fat Boy with its shotgun-style dual exhaust.
5182 South Arville St (two blocks south of the Orleans Hotel & Casino). Tel: (310) 536 6777. www.eagleriderlasvegas.com

Extraterrestrial Highway
State Route 375 stretches for 98 miles (158km) and passes close to Area 51, the world's most secret air base where ET hunters claim that UFOs are tested and flown. Stop for a snack at the world-famous Little A'Le'Inn, but keep your eyes skyward!
Nevada Route 375, Rachel, NV. The ET Highway is noticeably marked. Tel: (775) 729 2515. www.littlealeinn.com. Most tour operators offer Area 51 packages.

Fish Vegas
Chartered fishing trips on Lake Mead with master guide Captain Mike.
1547 Irene Drive, Boulder City. Tel: (702) 293 6294. www.fishvegas.com

Forever Resorts
This tour company offers boat charters, resorts and lodging, fishing and rafting cruises, and conference facilities around the Colorado River, Lake Mead and throughout the US.
www.foreverresorts.com

Grand Canyon Tour Company
Try the spooky Ghost Town and Gold Mine tour, or a selection of air, bus, helicopter, hiking or train tours that include the Grand Canyon, Lake Mead and the Hoover Dam.
Tel: (702) 655 6060. www.grandcanyontourcompany.com

Lake Mead Cruises
Voted by *Nevada Magazine* readers as the 'Best Adventure Tour Company in Nevada'. Cruises aboard their Mississippi-style paddle wheelers include a midday sightseeing cruise, an early dinner cruise and a dinner dance cruise. They also cater for weddings.
PO Box 62465, Boulder City. Tel: (702) 293 6180. www.lakemeadcruises.com

Las Vegas Boat Harbor Inc

This family business has operated on Lake Mead since 1957 and offers year-round boating, a café and a marine and tackle store. Powerboats, pontoon boats and jet-skis are all available to hire. This is the closest marina to Las Vegas.
490 Horsepower Cove, Boulder City.
Tel: (702) 293 1191.
www.boatinglakemead.com

Las Vegas Mini Grand Prix

Ten adults (aged 16+) can race around the longest go-kart track in Nevada, while their positions are displayed on an electronic timing board. A Kiddie Kart track is also available for children.
1401 North Rainbow Blvd.
Tel: (702) 259 7000. www.lvmgp.com.
Open: Mon–Fri 11am–9pm, Sat–Sun 10am–9pm.

Las Vegas Motor Speedway

Hosting many high-profile race events, the $200-million Las Vegas Motor Speedway complex features a 2.4km (1½-mile) super speedway Tri Oval with a 4km (2½-mile) road course, along with a dirt oval, a paved oval, a dragway, a paved Legends Cars track, go-kart and off-road facilities.
7000 Las Vegas Blvd N.
Tel: (702) 644 4444. www.lvms.com

Maverick Helicopter Tours

With an exclusive landing area in the Grand Canyon, Maverick offers several tours of the canyon as well as night flights over Las Vegas.
6075 Las Vegas Blvd S. Tel: (702) 261 0007. www.maverickhelicopter.com

Neptune Divers

Dive sites include the 13.7m (45ft) cruiser *Toruga* in the Boulder Islands dive park, the Cement Factory for more experienced divers, and the Scuba Park, which has seven underwater sites, including a sailing boat, cement tube and truck cab.

You'll find good boating conditions on Lake Mead

5831 East Lake Mead Blvd.
Tel: (702) 452 5723.
www.nevada-scuba.com

Red Rock Climbing Center

This indoor climbing centre provides 836sq m (9,000sq ft) of climbing space and caters for beginners and advanced climbers, offering group lessons or personal tuition.
8201 W Charleston Blvd #B.
Tel: (702) 254 5604. Open: Mon–Fri 10am–10pm, Sat & Sun 9am–9pm.
www.redrockclimbingcenter.com

Richard Petty Driving Experience

Not within every visitor's budget, this is strictly for racing-car fans. Ride along in a stock car, driven by a professional instructor, try eight laps on your own in a Winston Cup car, or choose 16- to 80-lap advanced programmes, all with tuition.
6975 Speedway Blvd, Unit D-106.
Tel: (800) BE-PETTY.
Open: Mon–Fri 8.30am–7.30pm, Sat & Sun 10am–4pm (EST).
The booking office is on the east coast of the United States.

Rocky Trails

Adventurous tours that include ATV quad four-wheeler tours, horse riding, kayaking below Hoover Dam, rafting, hiking in Red Rock Canyon and mountain biking.
1930 Village Center Circle 3–155.
Tel: 1 (888) 892 5380.
www.rockytrails.com

FURTHER INFORMATION

Grand Canyon National Park.
www.nps.gov/graca

Red Rock Canyon National Conservation Area. *Tel: (702) 363 1921.*
www.redrockcanyonlv.org

Spring Mountains National Recreation Area.
Tel: (702) 873 8800. www.fs.fed.us/htnf

Valley of Fire State Park. *Tel: (702) 397 2088.*
www.parks.nv.gov

See pp114–27 for more details of these areas.

Sky's The Limit

The largest indoor climbing centre in Nevada, offering 1,300sq m (14,000sq ft) of climbing walls for all levels. It also provides a guide service for those wishing to explore the outdoor ranges in the area.
1270 Calico Drive, Calico Basin.
Tel: (702) 363 4533.

Sundance Helicopters

After being picked up in a limo at your hotel, you fly over the Strip, out over Lake Mead and the Hoover Dam, before landing on a plateau within the Grand Canyon, for a picnic.
Tel: (702) 736 0606.
www.sundancehelicopters.com

Health clubs and spas

Las Vegas is not all about late nights and all-you-can-eat buffets. You can also pamper yourself in the city by visiting a health spa. Daily prices range from $15 to $50 but there may be discounts on offer for resort guests, and spa packages are often available when you arrange your hotel booking.

Canyon Ranch Spa Club

Claiming to be one of the largest day spas in the world, the Canyon Ranch includes the unique Aquavana aquathermal relaxation suites, three single-sex ones where bathing suits are optional and three mixed-sex where swimwear is required. There's also a 12m (40ft) indoor rock wall.

Venetian Resort Hotel & Casino, 3355 Las Vegas Blvd S. Tel: (702) 414 3606. Open: daily 6am–8pm.

The MGM Grand Spa

There's a wide range of treatments here, with several signature treatments among them, including an Australian Aboriginal-style massage. There are Ayurvedic therapies too.

MGM Grand, 3799 Las Vegas Blvd S. Tel: (702) 891 3077. Open: Mon–Thur 6am–7pm, Fri–Sun 6am–8pm.

The fitness centre at the Nurture spa at Luxor

Nurture at Luxor

The Nurture Spa offers several de-luxe massage treatments, including one for expectant mothers and a Lomi Lomi massage, inspired by Hawaiian shamanic rituals.

Luxor Hotel & Casino, 3900 Las Vegas Blvd S. Tel: (1800) 258 9308. Open: 6am–8pm.

Qua Baths & Spa at Caesars Palace

The Qua's unique selling point is its approach to what it calls social spa-ing, though you can have individual treatments too. Being at Caesars Palace, the style is modelled on the more communal nature of the Roman baths.

Caesars Palace, 3570 Las Vegas Blvd S. Tel: (702) 731 7776. Open: daily 6am–8pm.

The Reliquary Water Sanctuary & Spa

The spa at the Hard Rock gathers together treatments from all over the world. You feel like a pampered rock star, with massages from Russia, Sweden and Thailand, plus other treatments from Fiji, and a jokingly named 'Heavy Metal Wrap'.

Hard Rock Hotel & Casino, 4455 Paradise Rd. Tel: (702) 693 5520. Open: daily 6am–10pm.

Spa Mandalay

The huge Spa Mandalay offers special spa treatments for young adults aged 13–17, including facials, pedicures and manicures, while adults can enjoy the redwood sauna and eucalyptus steam room.

Mandalay Bay Resort & Casino, 3950 Las Vegas Blvd S. Tel: (1877) 632 7300. Open: daily 6am–8.30pm.

Spa by Mandara

Based at the Paris, the Mandara's theme is an Asian-European fusion, and treatments include a romantic 'Paris for Lovers' treatment in one of the six rooms reserved for couples.

Paris Las Vegas, 3655 Las Vegas Blvd S. Tel: (702) 946 4366. Open: daily 6am–7pm.

The Spa at Monte Carlo

This elegant spa offers massages, body scrubs, wraps, waxing, facials and detox treatments. Amenities include whirlpools, saunas, steam rooms and relaxation room, as well as a fitness centre and full-service salon.

Monte Carlo, 3770 Las Vegas Blvd S. Tel: (702) 730 7590. Open: daily 6am–9pm.

The Spa at Wynn

Like the hotel itself when it opened, the Spa at Wynn has to do something special. It has 45 treatment rooms in a vast area, half as big again as many other Vegas spas. Try the Good Luck Ritual, a 50-minute custom massage using Thai oils and herbs.

Wynn Las Vegas, 3145 Las Vegas Blvd S. Tel: (702) 770 3900. Open: daily 9am–7pm.

Children

Over the years, Las Vegas has grown as a family-friendly environment. Free attractions such as the MGM Lion Habitat or the Mirage Volcano will draw crowds of all ages, but the city does not claim to be marketing to children. As visitor numbers have increased, over 10 per cent of tourists are under the age of 21 and too young to indulge in the county's main source of revenue.

The city has been described as hospitable to families, but has not made any determined effort to encourage them in its promotional material, although there are many attractions, several suitable resorts and plenty of childcare facilities to make your stay enjoyable for the whole family.

Adults must accompany children under 12 to shopping centres and games arcades, even if they are in a group, and under-16s should not be out alone. On the Strip, there is a 9pm curfew for under-18s, so they must not be out and about after this time unless they are accompanied by a parent or guardian.

AGE RESTRICTIONS

There are strict gaming laws in Las Vegas. Visitors under the age of 21 are prohibited from loitering in or around any area where any licensed gambling is conducted, and cannot play, place bets or collect winnings. The legal age for the consumption or purchase of alcohol is also 21.

Hotels

Family-friendly resorts include Circus Circus, with its **Adventuredome Theme Park**, live circus acts and arcades, and the MGM Grand, with its free **Lion Habitat** and **Youth Activity Center** for guests. The Mandalay Bay has its **Shark Reef** as well as a beach. The Four Seasons will child-proof your room for you before you check in, while the Excalibur features the **SpongeBob SquarePants 4-D Ride** as well as the exciting dinner show *Tournament of Kings*, jugglers, entertainers and a court jester's stage in the Medieval Village. New York-New York offers the Manhattan Express roller coaster and arcades, while teens will enjoy the Speedway Motion Rides at the Sahara.

Most of the resorts have their own swimming pools – ideal if your kids are water babies – but it's always worth checking before booking.

Resorts not suitable for children include the Bellagio, which does not allow any visitors under the age of 18 to enter its premises, Caesars Palace, the Hard Rock Hotel, Riviera, Stardust and the Palms. Although the Palms does offer childcare facilities, the hotel attracts many stag parties, and promotes an adult theme throughout, so bear this in mind before booking.

Childcare facilities

Kids Quest! facilities can be found in the Palms and the Station casino group for children aged from 6 weeks to 12 years. Activities include its Ballocity Adventure game, spiral slides, ball pits, non-violent video entertainment

Kids Quest! *Available at all the Station Casinos. Tel: (1 800) 941 1007 or visit www.kidsquest.com*
Kid's Tyme Centers. *The Orleans, 4500 W. Tropicana Ave. Tel: (702) 365 7111; the Southcoast Hotel and Casino: 9777 Las Vegas Blvd S. Tel: (702) 796 7111.*
Camp Hyatt. *Hyatt Regency, 101 Montelago Blvd, Lake Las Vegas. Tel: (702) 567 1234.* Many resorts can arrange outside babysitting services.

games, arts and crafts, and virtual karaoke.

In the Orleans and the South Coast casinos, **Kid's Tyme Centers** offer multi-level jungle gyms, movie rooms,

The 10.5m (35ft) long Tyrannosaurus Rex even roars at onlookers

coin-free arcade rooms, the latest PlayStation, Nintendo and Wii games, and much more for a modest daily fee for children aged from 3 to 12 years. The centres are open every day of the year. The Hyatt at Lake Las Vegas offers **Camp Hyatt** for ages three to nine years, with activities that include outdoor games, swimming and water slides, arts and crafts, and toad and lizard hunting.

Family entertainment

Every hotel on the Strip is an attraction in itself, and, unless you exhaust the whole family by walking, a simple sightseeing trip can last for days. Enjoy the warm climate in the magnificent hotel pools in Las Vegas, or experience the best views of the city from the top of the Stratosphere or the *Eiffel Tower Experience* at Paris, then relax and take a gondola ride at The Venetian.

There are thrill rides, simulated rides and virtual reality attractions all over Las Vegas. At Neonopolis you can journey through time and space with the newly opened **Star Trek: The Experience** (*see p77*). Heart-stopping thrill rides include the Big Shot, Insanity – The Ride and X Scream at the **Stratosphere** (*see pp55–6*), the Manhattan Express at New York-New York (*see p34*) or Speed – The Ride at the Sahara (*see pp103–4*). Height restrictions apply on some of these rides.

For arcade games visit the Carnival Midway at Circus Circus (*see p176*), the Sports Zone arcade at the Hilton or GameWorks on the Las Vegas Strip (*see p176*).

All the family will love seeing the celebrities at **Madame Tussaud's Las Vegas** (*see p51*), seeing the impressive **Auto Collections** at the Imperial Palace Hotel (*see p56*) or visiting **Siegfried & Roy's Secret Garden** and **Dolphin Habitat** at the Mirage (*see p49*). At the NASCAR Café in the Sahara Hotel, family members can compete against one another in an exhilarating simulation of a 355kph (220mph) speedway experience (*see pp103–4*). Take a tour of the **Ethel M Chocolate Factory and Cactus Garden**, only 15 minutes away from the Strip (*see p176*), or the **Lied Children's Museum**, north of Las Vegas Boulevard (*see p177*).

Many of the family attractions in Las Vegas are free, such as the famed *Masquerade Show in the Sky* at the Rio (*see p157*) and the world-class street entertainers in the **Grand Canal Shoppes** at The Venetian (*see p51*). Children will also be captivated by the talking statues at the **Forum Shops** in Caesars Palace (*see pp40–41*). After dark the whole family can enjoy the *Fountains of Bellagio*, the **Mirage Volcano** or the Downtown **Fremont Street Experience** (*see pp38, 49 & 74–6*).

Attractions for children

In and around Las Vegas there are plenty of attractions that children will find fascinating, and many of them are free. Most hotels also offer games areas, such as Carnival Midway at Circus Circus and the Coney Island Emporium in New York-New York. *See pp102–6 & 157 for more attractions.*

Speed – The Ride winds around the Sahara

Adventuredome Theme Park

Fun for all ages, including a roller coaster, bumper cars, funhouse and virtual-reality zones housed within the largest indoor theme park in the world (*see p102*).

Circus Circus Hotel & Casino, 2880 Las Vegas Blvd S. Tel: (702) 794 3939. Open: Mon–Thur 10am–9pm, Fri & Sat 10am–midnight, Sun 10am–9pm. There are height restrictions on some of the rides. All-day passes available: prices depend on height.

Bonnie Springs Old Nevada

An hour outside Las Vegas and you're into the real Nevada desert, and Bonnie Springs Old Nevada is a collection of attractions with a Wild West theme situated in that harsh landscape (*see also p129*). For children, there's a petting zoo, where they can get up close to not just the more usual goats, deer and llamas, but even a Texas long-horned steer and a buffalo too. Also at Bonnie Springs is an old Western town with saloon and shops and even a cemetery. There's a chance to go horse-riding as well if you wish. Check the website or phone for the times of the various guided horseback rides into the desert, a world away from the neon lights of Las Vegas.

1 Gunfighter Lane, Blue Diamond, Nevada. Tel: (702) 875 4191. www.bonniesprings.com. Open: Wed–Sun 10.30am–6pm (summer), Wed–Fri 11am–5pm, Sat & Sun 10.30am–5pm (winter). Admission charge.

Ethel M Chocolate Factory & Cactus Gardens

Who can ask for more than a free tour of a chocolate factory? The botanical gardens also feature over 350 species of desert flora.

2 Cactus Garden Drive, Henderson. Tel: (702) 433 2500. www.ethelschocolate. com. Open: daily 8.30am–7pm. Free admission.

GameWorks

Including a 23m (75ft) rock-climbing pillar, video games, interactive entertainment and refreshments, this is one of the best arcades on the Strip.

3769 Las Vegas Blvd S. Tel: (702) 432 4263. Open: Sun–Thur 10am–midnight, Fri & Sat until 1am. Free admission, games priced individually.

Las Vegas Mini Grand Prix

Miniature racing cars, fun slides, a mini roller coaster and go-karts keep children and teens entertained for hours.

1401 North Rainbow Blvd. Tel: (702) 259 7000. Open: Mon–Fri 11am–9pm, Sat & Sun 10am–9pm.

Lied Discovery Children's Museum

Education through play. Learn about gravity with weight boots, compose music and put mathematics to use among many interactive activities.

833 Las Vegas Blvd N. Tel: (702) 382 3445. Open: Tue–Fri 9am–4pm, Sat 10am–5pm; Sun noon–5pm. Admission charge.

M&M's World

Features M&M merchandise, a 3D film, the M&M Academy – and offers every colour M&M in production.

Showcase Mall, 3785 Las Vegas Blvd S. Tel: (702) 736 7611. Open: Sun–Thur 9am–11pm, Fri & Sat until midnight. Attractions run 10am–6pm, Fri & Sat until 8pm. Free admission.

Midway

Carnival games for all the family, along with virtual-reality and interactive games. There are plenty of prizes to win, too.

Excalibur Hotel & Casino, 3850 Las Vegas Blvd S. Tel: (702) 597 7700. Open: daily 10am–midnight, Fri & Sat 10am–1am. Free admission, games priced individually.

Children

World of Coca-Cola, GameWorks and M&M's World on the Strip

An ever-evolving city

Where did they go? The Dunes, the Sands, the Desert Inn? These monarchs of the Las Vegas Strip are now lost in the clutches of developers. The original Strip hotels are disappearing from Las Vegas at a dramatic rate, as the city constantly rewrites its future in tourism.

The first hotel on the Strip, El Rancho, was lost in a fire in 1960, while the Dunes was 'imploded' (demolished) in October 1993, the Landmark in November 1995, and, after 50 years on the Strip, the Desert Inn finally closed its doors in August 2000. On 25 December 1995, lights throughout Las Vegas were dimmed to mark the death of Dean Martin, but even the historic Sands hotel, famous for its Rat Pack summit, could not fight the development of the city and was demolished in November 1996. The Venetian now stands on the site.

A hotel implosion is an attraction quite unique to Las Vegas. Hotel rooms are filled across the city as people check in to witness the event. Then, on the date of destruction, nearby streets are cleared and a dazzling display of fireworks and dynamite marks the demise of another Las Vegas landmark.

However, the city's ability to evolve has created a progressive and unrivalled tourist destination. As new hotels are built, older hotels are constantly being refurbished to maintain the luxurious Las Vegas standards. The 40-year-old Hacienda was replaced by the exotic Mandalay Bay, the old Desert Rose Motel made way for the Monte Carlo, and the Bellagio replaced the Dunes in 1996. Every new resort seems more impressive, more alluring and more expensive than its predecessors, creating an ever-changing panorama for the repeat visitor.

The opening of Steve Wynn's $2.7 billion Wynn Las Vegas in 2005 was a celebratory affair, coinciding as it did with the city's centenary, just 100 years since the first plots of land were sold at auction. Since then the world's economy has taken a big downturn, and Vegas has not been immune to its effects. Some planned projects have been put on hold, yet still the place changes. The recent ambitious CityCenter project opened in December 2009, adding even more stylish hotels to the Vegas skyline, including the Mandarin

Oriental, the ARIA Resort & Casino, and the Vdara Hotel & Spa, with the Harmon Hotel & Spa being the latest hotel to open: not bad, for an economy in recession.

Compared to other metropolitan areas, Las Vegas is an infant city. It is still growing, still evolving – and most welcoming to any visitors who are keen to chart its progress.

The non-gaming, boutique Harmon Hotel & Spa is the newest Las Vegas hotel to open

Practical guide

Entry requirements

Citizens of Australia, New Zealand, Ireland and the UK (as well as citizens of most western European countries and Japan) need only a valid machine-readable passport to enter the USA if their stay is less than 90 days, they have a return ticket and have arrived on an airline participating in the visa-waiver programme (most major carriers). Make sure that your visa-waiver form includes the full address of your first night's accommodation. If your passport was issued after 26 October 2005 and contains a non-digital photograph, you will be excluded from the visa-waiver programme. Canadian and Mexican citizens also now need a passport. Citizens of South Africa and most other countries must present a passport and tourist visa. There is now an extra check when you arrive at a US airport – a photograph plus fingerprinting.

Route 66 road sign

Travellers who require visas should obtain them from a US consulate or embassy in their country of residence, as they are difficult to obtain elsewhere. In the UK your Thomas Cook travel consultant can advise.

Unless you are flying directly to Las Vegas, it's likely that you will fly into a gateway city first. This initial stop will be where you clear immigration and customs. Ensure that your visa-waiver form and customs declaration are completed correctly when you leave the plane, as immigration officials are known for their lack of patience. Details can be found in most airline magazines, and flight attendants will also be able to advise you. Once you have cleared immigration, you pick up your luggage and proceed to US Customs. If you have a connecting flight your luggage will be re-checked after customs.

General airport information for McCarran International:
Tel: (702) 261 5211.
www.mccarran.com

Children and age limits

You must be over 21 to gamble and drink alcohol, and these rules are strictly enforced. Under-21s are also prohibited from loitering around casino areas, but there are several activities and entertainment centres for this age group, along with babysitting and childcare facilities for younger children.

Climate

Las Vegas has an arid climate, with average humidity around 29 per cent and 320 days of desert sunshine each year. In the winter after the sun sets, or even in the shade, Las Vegas can be quite cold, so pack a jacket or extra layer. The same applies when visiting hotels.

The air conditioning inside the resorts can make it seem very cold compared to the heat outside, so take an extra layer or you may be forced back outside to warm up.

Consulates and embassies

Australia: *150 East 42nd St, 34th Floor, New York, NY 10017-5612. Tel: (212) 351 6500.*
Canada: *1251 Avenue of the Americas, NY 10020. Tel: (212) 596 1783.*

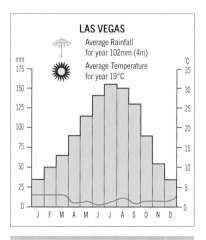

LAS VEGAS

Average Rainfall for year 102mm (4in)

Average Temperature for year 19°C

WEATHER CONVERSION CHART

25.4mm = 1 inch
°F = 1.8 × °C + 32

TRAVEL BASICS

- Las Vegas is Pacific Standard Time (GMT minus 8 hours).
- Electricity. The power supply is 110/120 volts AC. You will need a US mains adaptor and it is preferable to use dual-voltage electric razors and similar devices. There are hairdryers in most hotel rooms.
- You can post international mail from centres in most hotels. See the Yellow Pages for a main post office if you need one.
- Clean public toilets or restrooms can be found in all hotels and establishments throughout the city.
- Take ID. You may need a photo ID to use your credit card or prove that you are over 21. It is not advisable to carry your passport around everywhere with you, but a photocard driving licence would be ideal.

Republic of Ireland: *Ireland House, 345 Park Ave, 17th Floor, New York, NY 10154-0037. Tel: (212) 319 2555.*
UK: *845 Third Ave, NY 10022. Tel: (212) 745 0200.*

Conversion tables

See p187.

Crime prevention and safety

Do not carry more cash than you will need. Store valuables, travel documents and passports in the safe in your hotel room, if there is one available, or ask at the hotel desk for a safety deposit box.

If you have been lucky enough to win at the tables, try not to draw too much attention to your cash bonus. If you win a large amount ask the cashier for a cheque. They can also supply security if you feel it is needed. Security is high in the casinos and on the Strip, and it is generally safe for tourists, but take all the precautions that you would in any major city and do not flaunt jewellery or valuables.

If you are driving, avoid using dark hotel car parks at night, and always use the hotel main entrances, particularly if you are a woman travelling alone. Place valuables out of sight and locked in the trunk (boot).

If you think someone is following you contact hotel security immediately. The same applies if you think there has been an unauthorised entry to your hotel room. Always ensure that your hotel room is locked when you leave and immediately report any theft or mugging to the police.

When you arrive in your hotel room, always read the fire evacuation notice on the inside of the door and make sure you are aware of where the emergency exits are located. The huge Vegas resorts are easy to get lost in at the best of times, so you do not want any added confusion in an emergency.

There are many street canvassers in Las Vegas, and the best advice is to ignore them. Their material may offend you but their actions rarely pose a threat to visitors. If you want to give money to people begging on the street, the choice is yours, but your money may be better spent if you donate it to a street charity.

Despite the adult themes in Vegas, prostitution is illegal.

Customs regulations

Hand your customs declaration form to Customs. It should list all things brought into the USA, whether gifts for others or not. There is no limit to the amount of cash or traveller's cheques you may bring in or take out. Prohibited items include fresh meat, fruit, drugs (other than prescribed) and plants. Duty-free allowances for travellers aged 21 or more are: 200 cigarettes or 50 cigars, 2 litres of table wine and 1 litre of spirits. Travellers aged 18–21: no spirits allowed.

Driving in Las Vegas

You must be over 25 years of age to rent a car in Las Vegas. There are kiosks at the airport, but beware of hidden taxes charged on this type of rental. Booking a car before you leave home, or from your hotel or a rental depot away from the airport, will be cheaper.

You will need a driving licence and credit card to book a car. Be aware that if you visit Las Vegas during peak season, or when there is a special event or leading convention in town, car availability may be just as scarce as accommodation.

There are free parking facilities in most hotels, but even if valet parking is free you should always tip a couple of dollars. Unless you use the back roads to all the Strip hotels you may find yourself caught up in constant traffic on Las Vegas Boulevard. The worst places to cross the Strip are Tropicana Avenue, Spring Mountain Road and Sahara

Driving on the Strip can be tricky at peak times

Elephant fountain at Mandalay Bay

Avenue, which connect with Interstate 15, so avoid these intersections. The Desert Inn Road is the easiest way to cross the city.

Pay attention to speed limits and wear your seat belt at all times.

National/Statewide car rental companies

Avis. *Tel: (800) 230 4898. www.avis.com*
Dollar. *Tel: (800) 800 3655.*
www.dollar.com
Hertz. *Tel: (800) 654 3131.*
www.hertz.com

Las Vegas car rental companies

Enterprise Rent-A-Car. *Tel: (702) 795 8842. www.enterprise.com*
Sav-Mor Rent-a-Car. *Tel: (702) 736 1234. www.savmorrac.com*
US Rent-A-Car. *Tel: (702) 798 6100. www.us-rentacar.com*

Valley Xpress. *Tel: (702) 457 3728.*
www.valleyxpress.com

Electricity

The standard electricity supply is 110 volts (60 cycles). You may have to bring an adaptor to convert. Sockets take plugs with two flat pins. Appliances without dual voltage capability will also need a transformer. If in doubt, ask at your hotel desk.

Emergencies and emergency phone numbers

In an emergency, phone *911*, then ask for the service you require.

Health

Although Las Vegas is a thriving metropolitan city, it is still in the middle of the desert and you may take time to acclimatise to the heat. Drink plenty of water and always ensure you carry water with you while you are walking around. The most cost-effective way of buying water is in drugstores such as Walgreen's or in supermarkets as it can be very expensive in hotel food outlets and bars. The water in your hotel room is filtered and safe to drink but not pleasant. If you drink alcohol your chances of dehydration are severely increased.

Make sure that your skin is not exposed to the sun. Cover up with light clothing, wear plenty of sunblock and bring sunglasses. Sun can easily penetrate through clouds, so do not be fooled by overcast weather. The air is extremely dry, so wear lip balm, take advantage of the free moisturisers supplied with the toiletries in your hotel room, and contact lens wearers should bring extra solution.

Pack comfortable shoes as you could find yourself walking a long way as you explore the Strip. If you have any difficulties walking, you will also want to ensure that your hotel room is conveniently located close to a lift.

With the combination of the dry desert air and construction in this growing city, if you suffer from asthma or dust allergies, you might be severely affected and may not be able to stay in Vegas for more than a few days before it gets the better of you. Hay fever may also be a problem, particularly if you have an allergy to sagebrush.

Before you leave, make sure that you have medical insurance cover for at least $1 million. Take a credit card, as you will have to pay a fee to visit a doctor and may incur pharmaceutical costs on top. You will have to claim these expenses back from your insurance company when you return, so keep all your receipts. If the treatment is serious and likely to be expensive you will need to contact your insurance company directly, so make sure you take all the appropriate details and contact numbers with you.

If you are on any prescribed medication do not forget to take it with you on your trip and make sure that the supply will last for the length of your stay.

Medical help and emergencies
If you are taken ill, contact your hotel desk for information, or call a visiting doctor:
Inn-House Doctor Inc.
Tel: (702) 259 1616.
IN AN EMERGENCY CALL *911.*

Money matters
The unit of currency in the United States is the US Dollar ($), which is made up of 100 cents (¢).

Common coin denominations are:
1¢	Penny
5¢	Nickel
10¢	Dime
25¢	Quarter (meaning quarter dollar)

50¢ and $1 coins are also available, but are rare. Notes come in $1, $5, $10, $20, $50 and $100 denominations, but they are all the same size and colour so be careful not to mix them up. Higher notes are also available but are not readily accepted in many of the shops or establishments.

Most hotels will exchange your foreign currency and there are several exchange bureaus in Las Vegas.

It is advisable to bring traveller's cheques, which should be in US dollars. Traveller's cheques will be accepted as cash in most establishments (with photo ID) and most hotels or banks will exchange them for you, although taxi drivers will not accept them as payment. You will often need photo ID to use your credit card. Most major credit cards, such as AMEX, Carte Blanche, Diners Club, Discover, MasterCard (Eurocard, Chargex) and Visa (Barclaycard), will be accepted in Las Vegas. For a fee, you can also get a cash advance on your credit card, but it is more cost-effective to withdraw cash from an ATM. You will find cash points in most hotels, where you will be charged a small fee to your account but will benefit from a better exchange rate.

More city landmarks in New York-New York Hotel & Casino

Pedestrians

Take extra care when crossing the Strip. There are six lanes of busy traffic and drivers are often distracted by the many sights on Las Vegas Boulevard. Cross the Strip at pedestrian crossing points or use the bridges. Remember that traffic will be moving on the right-hand side of the road, and take care when walking across hotel entrances, as cars may be turning into them. Only cross roads when the 'WALK' symbol is displayed at pedestrian crossings and walk swiftly – you only have a short time to cross those six lanes.

Pharmacies

There are pharmacy counters in most supermarkets and drugstores. Walgreen's is conveniently located on the Strip, close to the junction of Charleston and Las Vegas Blvd S, and is open 24 hours.

Walgreen Drug Stores, 1101 Las Vegas Blvd S. Tel: (702) 471 6844.

Sustainable travel

Thomas Cook is a strong advocate of ethical and fairly traded tourism and believes that the travel experience should be as good for the places visited as it is for the people who visit them. That's why we firmly support The Travel Foundation, a charity that develops solutions to help improve and protect holiday destinations, their environment, traditions and culture. To find out what you can do to make a positive difference to the places you travel to and the people

CONVERSION TABLE

FROM	TO	MULTIPLY BY
Inches	Centimetres	2.54
Feet	Metres	0.3048
Yards	Metres	0.9144
Miles	Kilometres	1.6090
Acres	Hectares	0.4047
Gallons	Litres	4.5460
Ounces	Grams	28.35
Pounds	Grams	453.6
Pounds	Kilograms	0.4536
Tons	Tonnes	1.0160

To convert back – for example, from centimetres to inches – divide by the number in the third column.

MEN'S SUITS

UK	36	38	40	42	44	46	48
Rest of Europe	46	48	50	52	54	56	58
USA	36	38	40	42	44	46	48

DRESS SIZES

UK	8	10	12	14	16	18
France	36	38	40	42	44	46
Italy	38	40	42	44	46	48
Rest of Europe	34	36	38	40	42	44
USA	6	8	10	12	14	16

MEN'S SHIRTS

UK	14	14.5	15	15.5	16	16.5	17
Rest of Europe	36	37	38	39/40	41	42	43
USA	14	14.5	15	15.5	16	16.5	17

MEN'S SHOES

UK	7	7.5	8.5	9.5	10.5	11
Rest of Europe	41	42	43	44	45	46
USA	8	8.5	9.5	10.5	11.5	12

WOMEN'S SHOES

UK	4.5	5	5.5	6	6.5	7
Rest of Europe	38	38	39	39	40	41
USA	6	6.5	7	7.5	8	8.5

who live there, please visit
www.thetravelfoundation.org.uk

Telephones

To dial a local number ignore the area code (*702* in brackets) and dial the remaining seven digits directly. If you are calling from a hotel room you may have to enter a number to get an outside line before you dial. See the instructions printed on the top of your telephone.

For national calls and Canada, add a *1* before the area code (in brackets). For international calls, dial *011* followed by the country code (for example, *44* for the UK), then the area code (omitting the *0*), then the local number.

Country codes

Australia *61*	France *33*
Germany *49*	Ireland *353*
Netherlands *31*	Spain *34*
UK *44*	

The Luxor light beam is visible from space

If you are calling overseas from a public phone box, you will need at least $5–$6 in quarters and the operator may need to connect you. The operator can be reached by dialling *0*.

In hotels and casinos, public phone boxes are usually found by the toilets (or restrooms). They can also be found outside supermarkets and petrol stations and inside restaurants. Calling from your hotel room can be extremely expensive, even for national calls.

If you want to use your mobile phone in the United States, check with your service provider that your phone is suitable and that your service plan covers overseas travel. They will also advise you on the costs of these calls, which may be high. You can hire mobile phones when you visit: they are often available at car rental depots or your hotel can locate one for you. Again, calls will be costly.

The most economical way of making calls from a hotel room or public phone box is to use an international calling card. Hotel stores, drugstores and supermarkets sell them and they are usually available at most airports, but if you buy one before leaving home it will give you the opportunity to find the most cost-effective and suitable card for your visit.

Business services and Internet access

Most hotels have business centres, which can provide fax, photocopying or Internet facilities. You may also be able to access the Internet from your hotel room. There are several Internet cafés and access centres in Las Vegas, which usually charge between $5 and $12 per half-hour.

Tourist information

For tourist information, entertainment schedules and money-saving coupons there are several free magazines available throughout Las Vegas, such as *Las Vegas Today*, *Showbiz*, *Vegas Visitor* and *What's On*. The two main daily newspapers are the *Las Vegas Sun* and the *Las Vegas Review Journal*.

Las Vegas Information Centre, *3150 Paradise Rd. Tel: (877) 847 4858. Open daily 8am–5pm. www.visitlasvegas.com*

Other useful websites:
www.travelnevada.com
www.vegas.com

Travellers with disabilities

Las Vegas is a very accessible city for people in wheelchairs. If you have any specific accommodation needs, your hotel will be happy to help you in your booking. Most showrooms have assisted-listening devices and wheelchair access, as do restaurants and casinos, with slot machines at easy reach. Many airport shuttles are equipped with lifting devices, and if you are hiring a car you can obtain a disabled parking permit from the City of Las Vegas Parking Permit Office, *tel: (702) 229 6431, in advance.*

Index

Acknowledgements

Thomas Cook Publishing wishes to thank ETHEL DAVIES, to whom the copyright belongs, for the photographs in this book, except for the following images:

DREAMSTIME.COM 1 (Modi1980), 18, 54 (Rabbit 75), 29 (Ffooter), 45 (Bdingman), 56 (Geppe), 60 (lifesazoo), 75 (klotz), 91 (Minh Tang), 132 (Sporokop), 159 (Egomezta), 168 (Mehmet Dilsiz)
FLICKR 61 (Bludgeoner86), 64 (Dan4th), 79 (biskuit), 93 (MoToMo), 109 (adamjackson1984), 139 (Lana aka BADGRL), 145 (Marcin Wichary), 147, 155 (dherrera 96), 152 (Ethan Prater)
LAS VEGAS NEWS BUREAU 8, 23, 24, 25, 41, 47, 71, 98, 105, 110, 148, 161, 163
MGM MIRAGE 106, 143, 170
JON SULLIVAN (pdphoto.org) 5
US DEPT OF JUSTICE 17
WIKIMEDIA COMMONS 37, 149 (Alan Light), 53 (Zoo Fari), 141 (Nehrams2020), 151 (David Vasquez), 179 (Cygnusloop99)
WORLD PICTURES/PHOTOSHOT 14, 21, 67, 69, 86, 89, 97, 101, 104, 123, 166, 183

For CAMBRIDGE PUBLISHING MANAGEMENT LTD:
Project editor: Rosalind Munro
Typesetter: Donna Pedley
Proofreaders: Caroline Hunt & Kelly Walker
Indexer: Marie Lorimer

SEND YOUR THOUGHTS TO
BOOKS@THOMASCOOK.COM

We're committed to providing the very best up-to-date information in our travel guides and constantly strive to make them as useful as they can be. You can help us to improve future editions by letting us have your feedback. If you've made a wonderful discovery on your travels that we don't already feature, if you'd like to inform us about recent changes to anything that we do include, or if you simply want to let us know your thoughts about this guidebook and how we can make it even better – we'd love to hear from you.

Send us ideas, discoveries and recommendations today and then look out for your valuable input in the next edition of this title.

Emails to the above address, or letters to the traveller guides Series Editor, Thomas Cook Publishing, PO Box 227, Coningsby Road, Peterborough PE3 8SB, UK.

Please don't forget to let us know which title your feedback refers to!